Meditation on the Word
BRINGS THE MIND OF CHRIST

Meditation on the *Word*
BRINGS THE MIND OF CHRIST

Dr. Dorothy Sharpe

J. Kenkade
PUBLISHING®
Little Rock, Arkansas

Meditation on the Word Brings the Mind of Christ
Copyright © 2020 by Dr. Dorothy Sharpe

All rights reserved. No part of this book may be photocopied, reproduced, distributed, uploaded, or transmitted in any form or by any means, or stored in a database or retrieval system, without the prior written permission of the publisher.

J. Kenkade Publishing
6104 Forbing Rd
Little Rock, AR 72209
www.jkenkadepublishing.com
Facebook.com/jkenkadepublishing
J. Kenkade Publishing is a registered trademark.

Printed in the United States of America
ISBN 978-1-944486-86-0

Unless otherwise noted, scripture quotations are taken from the King James Version® Bible, Public Domain.
Used by permission. All rights reserved.

Scripture quotations marked (AMP) are taken from the Amplified Bible, Copyright © 1954, 1958, 1962, 1964, 1965, 1987 by The Lockman Foundation. Used by permission.

The views expressed in this book are those of the author and do not necessarily reflect the views of Publisher.

ACKNOWLEDGEMENTS

I thank God for His mercy, grace, wisdom, revelation knowledge, and favor on my life to write about His word of power.

I want to thank my husband, Bishop Eric Sharpe, for encouraging me to pursue my dreams and to tap into my hidden potential.

I want to thank my good friend, Mary Minton, who supported me all the way through with her giving and dedication to the vision.

I want to thank my friends in California and Chicago for their prayers, encouragement, and intercessory prayers. They let me know that God is no respecter of persons.

I want to thank the Holy Ghost for His miraculous blessings. He has revealed to me the "Mind of Christ". The love of the Father abides in my heart and soul forever.

I want to thank my family members for all their support.

I want to thank my children and grandchildren for all the encouragement they gave.

I want to thank all my friends, mentors, pastors, apostles, preachers, and teachers who poured inspiration and a helping hand to help me reach the success that God purposed in my life. They helped me see the vision clearly by lifting me up in their prayers.

May God bless each and every one of you, and may every need be met in your lives.

Praise the Lord.

TABLE OF CONTENTS

Introduction	13
Chapter 1: Meditate On God's Truth	17
Chapter 2: Daily I Meditate On The Law	19
Chapter 3: The Sweetness Of God	21
Chapter 4: My Heart Meditates	23
Chapter 5: The Acceptable Meditation	25
Chapter 6: Lord, Hear and Consider My Prayers	27
Chapter 7: Should I Meditate on Things?	29
Chapter 8: Answer Not Before Meditation	31
Chapter 9: The Wicked Meditate In Fear And Terror	33
Chapter 10: Meditate On The Works Of God	35
Chapter 11: I Meditate In Thy Precepts	37
Chapter 12: Thy Servant's Love Of Your Law	41
Chapter 13: I Have Respect Unto Thy Ways	43
Chapter 14: All Thy Works Are Excellent	45
Chapter 15: God's Love Watches Us In The Night	47
Chapter 16: Meditate Day and Night On His Law	49
Chapter 17: Lord, I Will Seek You Daily In Meditation	51
Chapter 18: I Will Meditate In Thy Field	53
Chapter 19: God Wants Our Whole Hearts	55
Chapter 20: Walking In Obedience	57
Chapter 21: God Is Our Trust	59
Chapter 22: Intimacy By Prayer	61
Chapter 23: True Repentance Is Mine	63
Chapter 24: The Holy Spirit Helps Us To Pray	65
Chapter 25: God Promises To Answer Prayer	67
Chapter 26: United Prayer	69
Chapter 27: Intercessory Prayer	71
Chapter 28: The Carnal Mind	73
Chapter 29: Let Your Mind Be Undefiled	75

Chapter 30: What Makes Your Thoughts Evil?	77
Chapter 31: The Lord Knows Our Thoughts	79
Chapter 32: We Possess Spiritual Minds	81
Chapter 33: We Have The Mind Of Christ	83
Chapter 34: Be An Example As Christ Jesus	85
Chapter 35: Thinking Soberly By Faith	87
Chapter 36: Think On The Things That Bring Peace	89
Chapter 37: Consider God's Provisions	91
Chapter 38: The Characteristics Of The Spiritual Mind	93
Chapter 39: God Sets Us Apart For Himself	95
Chapter 40: Let My Meditation Be Acceptable To God	97
Chapter 41: Thinking, Quietness, and Calmness	99
Chapter 42: Rest In The Lord	101
Chapter 43: Meditation In Silence	103
Chapter 44: Speaking Wisdom With An Excellent Spirit	105
Chapter 45: Our Words Have Power	107
Chapter 46: Seven Steps To Transform Your Thinking	109
Chapter 47: The Laws Of Poverty	119
Chapter 48: God's Four Laws Of Prosperity	121
Chapter 49: The Holy Spirit Witnesses To Us As Teacher, Leader, Spirit Of Truth, And Comforter	127
Holy Spirit As Teacher	129
Holy Spirit as Leader And Guide	130
Holy Spirit As The Life Giver	132
Holy As Spirit Of Truth	134
Holy Spirit As Our Comforter	135
The Purpose For The Anointing	137
Divine Ability Through The Anointing	138
The Force of the Anointing	140
Power Demonstrated By Love	141
Power To Become The Sons of God	142
God's Spiritual Blessings	143
God's Divine Favor	145
With Favor, God Hears Us	146

Prosperity Revealed To The Believers	148
Living In The Spirit (Prayer 1)	149
Living In The Spirit (Prayer 2)	150
The First Phase Of God's Revealing Knowledge	152
The Second Phase Of God's Revealing Knowledge	153
The Third Phase Of God's Revealing Knowledge	155
Our Earnest Expectations	156
Grace Abides In Weakness	157
Grace That Empowers Us	159
A Renewed Mind Trains The Tongue	160
The Spiritual Mind (Prayer 1)	162
The Spiritual Mind (Prayer 2)	163
The Spiritual Mind (Prayer 3)	164
About the Author	*167*
About J. Kenkade Publishing	*171*

*Change in any individual
must come through the "mind of Christ",
a revelation of who God's people are.*

INTRODUCTION

The mind of Christ reveals to us the anointed and appointed destiny of our lives. We can do nothing without the anointing. This is the administration of the Holy Ghost. The office of Holy Ghost is to define and clarify the mind of Christ to us and reveal to the household of faith the things seen and unseen in the natural when we activate our faith. Without faith, it is impossible to please God. We have His approval or confirmation on our walk, worship, and our daily lives.

The Holy Spirit gives us wisdom, direction, and comfort about the decisions we make in all areas of our lives: relationships, jobs, family, finances, and ministry. We are always able to get results when we allow the Holy Ghost to direct and reveal to us what the answer is to any situation. Without Him, we would fall flat on our faces. Some people have tried to live without that spiritual guidance and fallen, and great was that fall.

Meditation on the word day and night reveals to us creative ideas, strategies for life, and understanding to make great moves and investments toward success. We cannot be successful without the Holy Spirit guiding us every step of the way. Many say they can do what the Bible says and still be successful without divine guidance of the Holy Ghost, but they discovered that for the long haul, nothing succeeds without His direction. If you want longevity in life and all of God's benefits for life and prosperity, you must allow the Holy Ghost to take control of all areas of your life.

God loves us, and we have never thought on the real relationship we have with Him. God said, "Eye hath not seen, nor ear heard, neither have entered into the heart of man, the things which God hath prepared for them that love Him" (1 Corinthians 2:9).

We should be aware of the plans of grace and prosperity that awake us physically and spiritually because we love Jesus. God will reveal those things that He has for us by His Spirit. Only the Spirit of God knows what is hidden in the Spirit of man. 1 Corinthians 2:12 states, "Now we have received, not the spirit of the world, but the spirit which is of God; that we might know the things that are freely given to us of God."

We are full of the nature of God as redeemed believers. We cannot be natural if we want to live and know the wisdom of God. We should always look for the supernatural existence of God and be spiritual in our lifestyle. Knowing God spiritually gives us the mind of Christ. 1 Corinthians 2:15-16 states, "But he that is spiritual judgeth all things, yet he himself is judged of no man. For who hath known the mind of the Lord, that he may instruct him? But we have the mind of Christ." We meditate on the Word of God and compare spiritual things with spiritual, not what man teaches, but the guiding of the Holy Spirit.

God does not want us to walk as carnal in mind and spirit. He wants us to be spiritual in our walk because we have to be able to walk with Him. Walking with Christ in maturity will bring us into understanding that God's word is what keeps us aware of life and all the challenges it brings. The carnal man will say this is foolishness; he thinks the way he lives and exists is up to his smartness and clever ways of working within the system. He never realizes that God gives him the mind, energy, knowledge, and courage to go for the best life has to offer.

If he had mental problems, he would not be able to think of the better ways of life. If he had a disease, he would not have the energy nor the courage to push for the better ways of living because his body would be in pain and weak. We have to realize that all the wisdom, strength, and intellect we have comes from God because we are so fragile as human beings. We should be grateful and appreciative for the good things in this life because God gives us the strength and power to have life abundantly.

We are babes in Christ, as we can't handle certain things that happen to us. We begin to ask God why and beg for peace and help with whatever we need. 1 Corinthians 3:1-3 states, "And I, brethren, could not speak unto you as unto spiritual, but as unto carnal, even as unto babes in Christ. I have fed you with milk, and not with meat: for hitherto ye were not able to bear it, neither yet now are ye able. For ye are yet carnal: for whereas there is among you envying, and strife, and division, are ye not carnal, and walk as men.

Meditation brings us into deeper relationship with the Lord. When we meditate on His word day and night, He knows that we have a heart connection with Him and not just service with our lips. We are listening to Him and communicating with Him on a regular basis. He feels a deep connection with us. With any situation that disturbs us, He is always there to help solve it and bring forth a solution according to His will, and that is His word.

CHAPTER 1: MEDITATE ON GOD'S TRUTHS

God gives us understanding and revelation knowledge of His word. We hold that word in our hearts, and it goes deeper than the surface of our being. When we meditate on the word, the darkness flees, and the light of understanding shows up. Think of the time when you did not read the word or pray, and you didn't seek God for his revelation knowledge. You were living in confusion. The Bible says God is not the God of confusion, but of love, power and of a sound mind. Meditating on God's truths brings sound thinking and clear direction to you. The word of God keeps you under the protection of God and His divine presence. He is right there whenever you need Him in His word. His word prevents us from making wrong decisions and gives us insight into knowing when we do not know what to do.

The Holy Spirit comes in to teach us all truths. We can depend on Him for divine guidance every time. The key to living and walking in God's truths is obedience. We must be obedient to that word of insight or we may ultimately fall. Pray that God will reveal His truths plainly and that you will receive them every time.

When we follow the teachings of the Holy Ghost, God gives us revelation. The more we meditate on God's truths, the deeper our understanding of God and His purpose for us is made known by faith. The word is a guiding light that takes us out of darkness and gives us understanding and right standing with God.

Prayer: *Thank you, God, for the guidance of the Holy Spirit. I receive Your insights and the purpose You have for my life. Amen.*

CHAPTER 2: DAILY I MEDITATE ON THY LAW

Praying to God brings us closer to Him. We must fall in love with God's precepts. Life is in the word, and peace is in the word. When I pray, I feel that I have intimacy with God that makes me feel special. You know what? You are special with God because He is close to you at all times. Just as a husband and a wife would listen to each other, share their frustrations, and struggles and spend time together. This intimacy makes their relationship stronger.

There are no limits to true love. Knowing God brings us into an excellence of grace that we can never know with another human being. God extends Himself above all limits into the ages of time, and His love grows and does not weaken. He knows the number of strings of hair on our heads and all the tears we have ever cried. He counts the waves of the oceans and causes the world to turn on its axis. You can praise Him all day long, yet with Him time stands still.

His word is power, an eternal flame of perfection that quickens the spirit of us all. His word protects me from my enemies and consumes them throughout eternity. He quickens my spirit and brings life to my existence. His word stands firm as the heavens. As the psalmist says, "O', taste and see that the Lord is good, and His mercy endureth forever" (Psalm 34:8). By His testimonies, He has quickened me and granted me life in Him that explodes with peace, love, and joy. The love flows from God's testimonies to me as I testify to Him through prayer (Psalm 119:93-97).

Prayer: *Lord, hear my prayer and turn not Your face from me. I love Your testimonies. My life has no limits in You. I will long for You all the days of my life. Quicken my spirit, O' Lord, and hear my cries and be merciful to me. Amen.*

CHAPTER 3: THE SWEETNESS OF GOD

The Lord is clothed with honor and majesty. He is very great. He is a sovereign God. He stretches out the heavens as a curtain. He gives us water so deep – He sent forth springs and valleys, and He clothes the beasts of the field and the fowls of the air and set the boundaries for the waters.

My meditation of God shall be sweet. I will be glad in the Lord. He has created all things in His wisdom; he feeds the fowls and the creeping things. His blessings and provisions shall last forever. His glory is manifold, as is His lovingkindness. Bless the Lord for all His mighty works. Call on Him, o', my soul! He will ultimately deliver me from spoilers and unjust men. The earth is full of His riches. He will not allow me to be in lack. God wants His children to prosper forevermore.

He has given us the tides for seasons. Surely, He has determined a blessed season for all those who love and trust Him. God has created a time and destiny for man to walk in his work and his labor until the evening of his life. Evening may be the time in a man's life that he starts to see the fading of the sun, or it may be the time God grants us to enjoy the seasons of our lives.

God's glory shall endure forever; the Lord shall rejoice in His works. We meditate on Him and the sweetness of God's love. God's love is like the fruits of grace and essence of mercy. Bless thou, Lord, O', my soul. Bless His holy name.

Prayer: *Thank you Father for your gentle love and mercy. You feed me and clothe me and added blessing eternal to my seasons on earth. Your glory shall endure forever. Amen.*

CHAPTER 4: MY HEART MEDITATES

My heart will search out the wisdom of God, and He will bring revelation to my mind and spirit. I can discern by faith those unsearchable problems and situations that frustrate me.

God has given me a divine enabling to speak the word of faith in my heart and meditate on it and whatsoever the problem or task may be, it will be dissolved. I will not fear what man can do or any means he may use to try to cause me to fail for the word says that no weapon formed against me shall prosper (Isaiah 54:17).

My trust is in God, who provides all my needs. I will not trust man or his riches. God's riches are incorruptible, full of mercy and grace, and overflowing in wisdom that turns not to dust but endureth forever. All who trust in man and the riches of this world shall perish and be consumed by the grave, but the upright shall see no death. God shall deliver our souls from the power of the grave, for He shall receive us. The glory of God is better than the honor of men's increase for when men die, that trust in this world's glory means nothing. No one shall carry anything with Him; his glory shall not descend after Him.

Let me see the light of my Heavenly Father that I may dwell with Him forever and ever even until death. My

God's eternity is the glory we should seek that is the light of our true existence. We shall have dominion over the glory of the men from morning until night and their beauty shall be consumed in the grave (Ps 49:3-17).

Prayer: *Father, receive my meditation and show me my destiny that will bring Your work into the glory of Your everlasting plan. To please You is better than the honor and glory of men. Amen.*

CHAPTER 5: THE ACCEPTABLE MEDITATION

We operate in the power and the strength of our redeemer. The acceptable meditation is that of total dependency on God: His will, His provisions, His saving grace. Can you measure your own life or your destiny? None can measure the future or the plans laid out by God for our lives. We are at the mercy of our redeemer.

God's work spreads the layers of the sun, brushes the stars as the dust of light reflects our total being. God covers the earth like a blanket. He hears us as a trumpet sounds through the wind. Nothing is hidden from Him.

"The statutes of the Lord are right on, rejoicing the heart: the commandment of the Lord is pure, enlightening to the eyes. The fear of the Lord is clean, enduring for ever: the judgments of the Lord are true and righteous altogether. More to be desired are they than gold, yea, than much fine gold: sweeter also than honey and the honeycomb" (Psalm 19:8-10).

God will keep you from the devourer. He will protect you from secret sins that so easily beset us. God is pure and just, unveiled with love for his children. He has made us pure, just, and upright before Him. We are made righteous in his sight. Who can condemn us? We are innocent as little children in his sight. He has kept us from the great transgression by his act of love by his son Jesus. I am so overwhelmed.

Prayer: *Thank you, Father, allowing me to get into Your presence to give the meditation of my heart in Your word of praise. You are my strength and my redeemer. Amen.*

CHAPTER 6: LORD, HEAR AND CONSIDER MY PRAYERS

O' God, hear my cry early in the morning. I will lift up my voice, a prayer in my most holy faith. I will speak to God in tongue. Only He knows my heart and the meditations of my soul.

Hear me, Abba Father, for You know my inner parts. You know my concerns. You know my needs. Lord, I want what You want. Teach me to please you. What would you have me to do? Open the multitudes of Your mercy towards me that I may be faithful in all my doings. I can do nothing without Your approval. Confirm my ways in righteousness. Make Your way plain and clear before me because those who seek my hurt speak against me. They lay traps for my feet. Their hearts are destructive. Their thoughts create an open sepulcher against me. Hold them guilty and let them not prevail against me. Let their own strategies cause them to be ensnared with their own clever designs of wickedness. Set their traps by their transgression and the counsel they take against me. David began to plead with God and cry out, "Let Your servant, O' Lord, who trusts in You be victorious and full of joy. Let Your love shower us with mercy and grace and

Your plentiful blessings of love shield us from all unrighteousness. Encapsulate us with Your lovingkindness. Lord, we bless Your holy name forever for You are not a God who takes pleasure in wickedness, neither will the evil man dwell in Your sight.

Prayer: *Father, thank You for giving me the grace to overcome my enemies and the cares of this life, so that I may live victorious in Your favor and abundant life. Amen.*

CHAPTER 7: SHOULD I MEDITATE ON THINGS?

We must accept the sayings and teachings of God and refuse and deny the teachings of demonic servants of Satan. Meditate on the commands and teachings of God. We are to be examples to others: believers of God in word, in conservation, in charity, in spirit, in faith, and in purity.

Our words should be truth, full of grace and encouragement toward believers and strangers. Our conservation should be uplifting in truth and full of insight about God's promises. In spirit, we must recognize that God loves us all and has is no respecter of persons by race, creed, or color. In faith, we know that God promises us the blessings that will flow if we give out of a sincere heart. As to faith, we know that we cannot please God without faith and the just shall live and walk by faith. We trust God to fulfill His word towards us. In purity, we walk upright before all men in forgiveness and love that flows from heart to heart and breath to breath. These things we meditate on and teach.

We are to read the word and ask God for understanding. The Holy Spirit is our teacher, and He will guide us into all truths. We are to exhort the teachings of the Holy Spirit and follow His lead that we be not ashamed of the gospel but study to show ourselves approved by God and worthy of all acceptance by the saints.

We live by the doctrine of Jesus Christ. You know that the anointing carries the power and the authority to bring you into the favor and provisions of God. We are not to neglect the gift in us that is placed in us by the Holy Spirit. We give ourselves totally to these things and our prospering may be seen by all on Earth and in heavenly places. Yes, we meditate on these things.

Prayer: *Thank You, Lord, for Your truths and provisions that are given by Your promises. I am not ashamed of the gospel for it is the authority that brings us unto Your divine power. Amen.*

CHAPTER 8: ANSWER NOT BEFORE MEDITATION

God gives the power to speak to any situation. He gives the wisdom to speak the right answer before our adversaries. God knows all the answers; there is nothing too hard for Him to give us a solution. We must listen in our spirits to that quiet, still voice of the Lord that guides us to revelation of all matters.

Sometimes, we want to make our own defense for a problem, but God already has the answer before we are aware of it. Why put yourself through such heartache and despair when you only have to allow God's spirit to connect to your spirit and reveal to you the answer you should have?

God promises to help us in every matter of defense or accusation of Satan and his demonic crew. Matthew 10:19-20 states, "But when they deliver you up, take no thought how or what ye shall speak; for it shall be given you in that same hour what ye shall speak. For it is not ye that speak, but the Spirit of your Father which speaketh in you."

God will give us wisdom for our relationships, our marriages, our finances, even our mental and physical health. We will find the answer as we seek God for direction. There is no option, no other decision to make but to listen to the Spirit of God. God will lead you in the right direction every time. The Holy Spirit teaches us what to say on any matter at all times. He brings things to our remembrance; He always gives us peace. He teaches us all things in peace and comfort, as God has promised that He will guide us and abide with us at all times (Luke 21: 14-16).

Prayer: *Lord, You give me the courage and confidence to depend on Holy Spirit to lead and guide us, teach us, and comfort us at all times and for every situation we face in life. Amen.*

CHAPTER 9: THE WICKED MEDITATE IN FEAR AND TERROR

The world does not see what the believers see. God's people can see the unseen by faith. All things are possible to those who believe and trust God.

Seeing God and meditating in His presence makes you more like Him. God will show you a new life, new beginnings, new relationships, a new wife, a new husband, new jobs, and new ideas and strategies to solve any failings the evil one throws at you.

God will give you peace and not terror of heart when you act on faith and not only on sight. God's presence gives us restoration. He is a tabernacle that cannot and shall not be taken down; not one of the stakes thereof shall ever be removed, neither shall any of the cords thereof be broken. God's ways and words divinely guide us; we can do nothing in our own strength; but in Him and with Him, we can do all things. God is our King and our Deliverer. In Him, we live, move, and have our being.

The unbeliever walks in fear; they can see no good. They cannot see far off. They have no revelation of the now or things to happen in the future. They are filled with and live in darkness of this age.

God restores the believer. He restores us: body, mind, and spirit. He establishes us by the word of His power. We believe the promises of God. We are fully persuaded that all our needs are met by faith in Jesus Christ.

God will bring about a great awakening in your spirit. Isaiah 33:10 states, "Now will I arise, saith the Lord; now will I be exalted; now will I lift up myself." God is on our side. The Lord is on the side of the one who meditates on His laws and statutes by faith and do them.

Prayer: *Lord, I thank You for Your salvation and Your care for me. I need You to guide me in every step of my life. Without You, I would fall. Guide me by the power of Your might. Amen.*

CHAPTER 10: MEDITATE ON THE WORKS OF GOD

Do you remember what God did for you when you were out of the arc of safety? What kind of pit where you in? Were you a smoker, a drinker, or a whoremonger? God brought us out of our mess. He restored us to a right relationship with Him, grinning before great men.

The works of God's hand have delivered us from shame and doubt. We have no fear of what man can do, or what the evil one can do. We walk by the power of God's divine love. God's hands have shaped our lives. He gives purpose to your life. He gives stability to your relationships. He keeps you from doubts and mediocre living by His destiny plan for your life. We do not always see the work, but we know God is operating and executing His righteous judgments, bringing us closer to His plans He has set in order throughout the ages. The word tells us that we must lift up our inner selves to God, then He will meet us. Psalm 143:10 states, "Teach me to do Your will, for You are my God; let Your good Spirit lead me into a level country and into the land of uprightness.

God saves us from the distress and confusion of this world. He knows what we need and how to give us good things for His name's sake. He will destroy our enemies and keep us from destruction. He keeps us whole, intact, sober-minded, and full of His anointing. Scripture states, "Cause me to hear Thy lovingkindness in the morning; for in Thee do I trust: cause me to know the way wherein I should walk; for I lift up my soul unto Thee" (Psalm 143:8).

God hears us, and He answers your prayers. He is a faithful God. He justifies us by His righteousness.

Prayer: *Thank You, Father, for bringing my life out of trouble and freeing me from distress. You shall destroy those who afflict my inner self for I am Your child. Amen.*

CHAPTER 11: I MEDITATE IN THY PRECEPTS

Meditation on God's law uplifts and comforts us. We are not to get upset and discouraged by lifestyles and dealings of the wicked. God will not allow our feet to be snared or our purpose to fade. He is fulfilling His promises in your life right now.

Our lives must reflect what we believe. Daniel trusted God. He had no second thoughts about refuting the king about his meditation on God's law. Daniel did not hesitate to seek God for the answer and to worship God in times of peace and in the times of trouble. He was fully persuaded that God loved Him, no matter how dire the situation.

Some people use God for a last-minute fix. God knows your heart. The best way to rest in God's love and mercy is to worship Him at all times. Do not wait until the enemy comes in or some dramatic situation knocks at your door. Let God know that you worship Him just for who He is. Give Him worship, honor, and praise. All to God (Holy Spirit) commit daily to prayer and supplication with thanksgiving. Seek Him wholeheartedly as the word says, "Let my heart be sound in Thy statutes; that I be not ashamed" (Psalm 119:80).

God will give you a renewed heart and a renewed mind. We are to love the word and hide it in our hearts so that we sin not, as David did. Sin is what makes you ashamed. Sin causes guilt and depression.

So many people are beaten down by guilt that Satan has put on them simply because they have not allowed the washing of the word to penetrate their inner man. As Psalm 119:78-80 suggests, the proud and those who rebel against God will be ashamed. We as children of God are to meditate in His precepts (laws) and not be ashamed for He is faithful in His promises.

In the comfort of God's statutes, we rest. The word of God quickens us. Psalm 119:50 states, "This is my comfort in my affliction; for the word hath quickened me." We are revived, rejuvenated, and lifted by the word.

God's statutes excite us and cause us to lift up our hands and praise Him for He is good, and His mercies endureth forever. I will give supplication and attend to prayer; I will seek the Lord for He has promised.

He has promised me hope in times of trouble. He has promised comfort at a time of derision. The Lord loves me and causes me to take heed to His guidance. He gives you hope for today and tomorrow. I have faith and confidence, and I trust God to take care of all my needs according to His riches in glory. The spiritual comes before the natural. We are always looking for the natural before searching for what God's spirit has planned for us. I will meditate in God's statutes. Psalm 119:48 states, "My hands also will I lift up unto Thy commandments, which I have loved."

The commandments of God comfort me. They key me into the pathway of righteousness; they keep my feet from the path of destruction. I will meditate on Thy statutes as long as I live for they are life to me and my household. They are my testimonies, my buckle, and my shield. The intercession of God's statutes keeps me humble amidst the goodness of God. My enemies almost put me in despair, but God's statutes sustained me as I walked in His righteous judgments and sustaining grace (Psalm 119:48-55).

Prayer: *Father, I trust You to manifest in the way You would have me go. Keep my feet in Your sustaining pathway and shield me from all unrighteous doings. Amen.*

CHAPTER 12: THY SERVANT'S LOVE OF YOUR LAW

Many tribulations and false accusations have befallen me, but I meditate on the statutes of God. I delight in the word of my salvation. I delight in the laws that strengthen me and protect me from the reproach of my enemies.

I seek counsel from Your statutes. They stimulate me according to Your word. Psalm 119:25-35 states, "Princes sat and talked against me, but Your servant meditated on Your statutes. Those in high places plotted against my life, but Your statutes comforted me. I meditate and talk of Your great works and wondrous deeds. Lord, I know You will raise me up from any despair or attacks of the enemy. I have chosen Your way.

I have chosen the truth that You may grant me a prosperous life. O' Lord, put me not to disgrace. Enlarge my heart. I am full of Your love and grace. I love Your statutes. Teach me Your ways. Help me to understand all the revelations of Thy wisdom.

Teach me how to be full of Thy righteous judgments. I am thirsty for Your gentle mercies. I trust in Your word; it is a blanket to cover me from the storms of life. It is shelter that protects me from the boisterous winds. It is food for my soul that I may be filled with Your lovingkindness. Refute the rebel and arrogant one who talks against Your ordinances. Let them be a heap of nothingness.

I will praise You and love Your statutes. I am strengthened by the statutes of Your promises. I have comforted myself by Your salvation and statutes of old.

Prayer: *Lord, I love Your laws. They have sustained me and kept me from harm and the enemies of my soul. I will glory in Your revealed wisdom. Amen.*

CHAPTER 13: I HAVE RESPECT UNTO THY WAYS

Blessed are those who honor the Lord. Love of the word is precious to the Lord. God's ways teach us that obedience brings about a beautiful life, a life of peace where nothing is broken, and nothing is missing.

The word says in Psalm 119:15-16, "I will meditate in Thy precepts and have respect unto Thy ways. I will delight myself in Thy statutes; I will not forget Thy words."

How can you forget God's words? This is not a mental forgetfulness. This is a lack of hearing, obedience, and studying of God's word. This is a deliberate refusal to walk in the light and live being a doer of the word and not just a hearer. The Bible says we must put on Christ as a garment and live accordingly.

God wants us to keep the word in our eyes, ears, and our mouths. We must speak this word and keep it before us day and night according to Joshua 1:8. Even without God's words, the very essence of our spiritual and physical strength, we have His statutes to keep us from fear.

Let us read Psalm 119:39. It states, "Turn away my reproach which I fear: for Thy judgments are good." God's law is good for us. We need His statutes to face the wiles of Satan and win every time. God causes us to walk freely without fear in every area of our lives. His testimonies are a delight. You must love God's precepts. They guide our minds and hearts to do God's will and find His will for our lives. We shall love God's authority in determining our destiny.

We can speak boldly and say, "God will be blessing me and put His commandments in my heart; that is His delight." What did David say? "Thy word have I hidden in my heart, that I might not sin against Thee" (Psalm 119:11).

***Prayer:** Father, I will hide Your word in my heart. I know You will hear me, and I will not fear what man can do unto me. I will delight in Your word as my final law and authority. Amen.*

CHAPTER 14: ALL THY WORKS ARE EXCELLENT

Lord, Thy ways are divine, and Thy works are excellent. I will meditate on all Thy works and talk of Thy doings. Thy right hand of power has redeemed Thy people. Thou hath done wonders on land and in the waters. The sound of thunder and the visions of lightning hath declared Thy strength.

The earth trembles from the sound of thunder, the rumbling of God's power at work. The word declares in Psalm 77:19-20, "Thy way is in the sea, and Thy path in the great waters, and Thy footsteps are not known. Thou leddest Thy people like a flock by the hand of Moses and Aaron."

The way is before us even in our sanctuary. You have kept nothing from us. Your wisdom and grace envelope us. By praise and worship, we are connected to Your lovingkindness. We are Your instruments of great pleasure. O' Lord, remember our voices of thanksgiving and the pleading of our supplications.

God is at work in us to do His perfect will for His pleasure, according to Philippians 2:13. We are humble before Him. He does all things by His excellent mercies. His ways are unsearchable. His redemptive power covers His people. He is great, and He is wise. His right hand instructs us. He hears us when we call.

Lord, Your redemptive power gives us strength, and Your divine arm redeems all generations. Surely, You have provided divine mercies and wisdom that we can look to You as Abba Father. God, Your works are endowed with Your divine power.

Prayer: *O' God, lead us in the path of Your redemptive works. We need You to instruct us in every way to live. You are our Father who delivers us from all destruction by Your divine arm. Amen.*

CHAPTER 15: GOD'S LOVE WATCHES US IN THE NIGHT

Watch the works of God and see His glory and power in the days of your youth, and you will remember Him when night comes; not the night as in the time on a clock, but the "night" of your own maturity in the word and obedience to that word. In the maturity of God's praise, we become wiser and more satisfied in the fullness of God's spiritual joy. We are thankful for His divine support. He keeps our souls from the grasp of our enemies.

Give God an oath and keep it. Praise Him, as scripture says in Psalm 63:6, "…I remember Thee upon my bed, and meditate on Thee in the night watches."

I remember God. He is our helper. He protects from all hurt, harm, and danger. He causes us to rejoice because we follow after His precepts. God rejoices in those who swear by His glory. Their minds are made up, and their hearts are fixed. We are His chosen. My flesh, soul, and spirit thirsted after God. I desire to see His glory and His power.

Some have become liars; they are not speaking the blessings of God. They glory in vain things and their own deceit. I will trust God and lift up my hands of praise to Him. God sustains me; He satisfies me with good things.

My lips will forever praise Him, as it says in Psalm 63:5-6, "My soul shall be satisfied with marrow and fatness; and my mouth shall praise Thee with joyful lips."

Make a joyful shout unto the God of our salvation. He fights against the enemies of our souls (intellect, emotions). He will deal justly with the wicked. They all shall fall by His sword that cuts going and coming, which is the word of God.

Prayer: *O' Lord, thank You for divine protection. Thank You for being a watcher over my soul and spirit. What shall I render for all of Your lovingkindness and benefits? Amen.*

CHAPTER 16: MEDITATE DAY AND NIGHT ON HIS LAW

Listen to God and follow His teachings and His instructions, and you will be blessed. You will be happy, prosperous, and enlightened with revelations of the knowledge of God. You are the one who will be as the writer described in Psalm 1:2 – "But his delight and desire are in the law of the Lord, and on His law (the precepts, the instructions, and the teachings of God), He habitually meditates (ponders and studies) by day and by night."

What does it mean to "ponder"?

According to the Hebrew definition, it means to "weigh out mentally", "revolve", or "search out". We must ponder in our hearts the word of God and meditate deep in our thoughts that God's spiritual revelations will be revealed to us. The studying of God's word must be a daily, habitual thing. You must have the desire to feed your spirit and allow the studying and research of that word to bring joy to your heart. When you meditate on the laws of God, He is determined to grow you and mature you in his Kingdom ways with the meat of the word.

The ungodly are disobedient and living without God's protection. They have no substance; they are like the walking dead. They shall not stand in the congregation of the righteous. Psalm 1:6 (AMP) says, "For the Lord knows and is fully acquainted with the way of the righteous, but the way of the ungodly (those living outside of God's will) shall perish (end in ruin and come to naught).

The righteous shall bring forth fruit in due season and their living shall be manifested, growing by the power of God and whatsoever we do shall prosper.

Prayer: *Lord, thank You for blessing and prospering me and my family. I will be obedient to Your word and seek You day and night. I will listen to Your counsel and follow Your instructions so that I may be happy all the days of my life. Amen.*

CHAPTER 17: LORD, I WILL SEEK YOU DAILY IN MEDITATION

According to the Hebrew definition, "meditate" means to "murmur (in pleasure or anger)", to "ponder", "imagine", "mourn", "mutter", "roar", "speak", "talk", "study", or "utter".

The Lord lets us know in Joshua 1:8, "This book of the law shall not depart (leave) out of thy mouth; but thou shall meditate therein day and night, that thou mayest observe to do according to all that is written therein: for then thou shalt make thy way prosperous and then thou shalt have good success."

The Lord assures us that meditation on the word constantly will give us the victory in our lives. We cannot obtain success in life while overlooking the giver of the ability to succeed. God enables us through study, speaking and pondering on the word to gain the revelation we need to get the result He wants us to have. We cannot do anything outside of God's will in his word. God will be with us wherever we go. He is with us when we battle the enemies of our lives, such as: lack, fear, depression, worry, fear of rejection, fear of failure, and fear of not having enough. God is no respecter of persons. What He does for one, He will do for the other.

The Lord told Joshua to be strong and take courage. We can stand on the word, and God will work in us and enable us to obtain the victory. God keeps His promises. He tells us not to look one way or the other, just look at Him straight on. He doesn't want us to doubt, but to be full of wisdom, being obedient unto righteousness in order to have great success.

When God tells you something or promises you something, you know it will come to pass. Just believe and be strong, and God will show up in any and every circumstance.

Prayer: Lord, I thank You for the encouragement to be strong. I know that all Your promises are yes and amen. I know that our victory and prospering will be by Your word. Amen.

CHAPTER 18: I WILL MEDITATE IN THY FIELD

Sometimes we need to go out among the crowds to meditate. Some say the hustle and bustle of the world distracts us from fellowshipping with God. This complaint is only an excuse. Connecting with God only requires that we recognize Him in all that we do, and in all that we do, we do it as unto the Lord.

I will delight myself in the Lord and give Him my heart. Night and day, God causes us to rejoice in His word. Just as Elisha went out in the countryside to pray, I will find the Lord and stand in His rest. I will look out on the fields of His making and meditate on His word. I will lift up my voice and praise the Lord. I will mourn and mutter His words. Only He will hear me and make my heart glad. Truly I will bow down in prayer in the open country and sing songs of worship to my God.

Do not delay searching for the vision of God. Inquire after Him early and be blessed. Do not linger when God has called you for His plans. Your destiny is in His hand. Cry out to God and make your desires known. Let Him know your heart and put His will first in your life. God

will strengthen you; He will provide blessings untold.
God sees the end of a thing from the beginning. We are His masterpiece. He created us in His image. He has caused us to prosper in our way. His benefits are full of His glory. Genesis 24:56 (AMP) says, "But (the servant) said to them, 'Do not hinder and delay me, seeing that the Lord has caused me to go prosperously on my way'".
God knows our hearts, and He wants us to be faithful. We are to be good, faithful stewards of all He has given us charge over. We are His ambassadors of grace. He needs to be able to depend on us in every situation that is brought before us. Let us bow down in honor and prayer to our savior and Lord Jesus Christ.

***Prayer:** Lord, help me to be able to represent You in this world so that my life will cause the lost to give You their whole hearts.*
In Christ Jesus. Amen.

CHAPTER 19: GOD WANTS OUR WHOLE HEARTS

We are to love God totally with all our being, soul and might. We are to think on God and His goodness and mercy. We should never forget that God gave His only begotten son for us. Jesus paid the penalty for our sins. God gives us the might (the strength and power) to do all things. If it were not for God on our side, we would be lost and confused due to Satan's devices.

God gives us insight; He enlightens us about the ways of Satan. He gives us creative inventions and strategies to do what we don't know how to do. We are God's masterpiece, and He has a plan for us. We must walk in it, speak it, and decree it at all times. It is not about how we feel or what it looks like. God enables us to operate by the power of His might.

Obey the voice of God and follow his will. He will bless us and all our children. We will receive the benefits of Jesus because we are heirs of the promise. He promised Abraham the blessings, and He gave these same promises to his children. We are the seeds of Abraham.

He obeyed and believed God, and it was counted to Him as righteousness. We have the same blessed promises on our lives today as we receive those benefits by grace. The word revealed to us in Deuteronomy 30:6, "And the Lord your God will circumcise your heart and the heart of your descendants, to love the Lord your God with all your heart and with all your soul, that you may live."

God will avenge us to our enemies and put curses on them, but He will bless those who are faithful and believe. God made the covenant with Abraham, but He made those blessings and benefits available to us. All we have to do is receive what God has promised and walk in those promises.

Prayer: *Lord, I thank You for Your promises and making them available to me, my family, and those who believe and receive Your covenant principles.*
Amen.

CHAPTER 20: WALKING IN OBEDIENCE

The obedience of God's children gives them special privileges. We are envied by our enemies when we are obedient to God's word. I seek God's presence early in the morning. Early in the morning will I seek Him, and happy am I when I seek His face. His testimonies fill my heart with joy. I am amazed at the favor that God gives me. God has blessed you abundantly above all you can ask or think. God will keep us justified by His righteousness –not our righteousness but by the righteousness of God.

God reveals His will by His word. He makes known to us all that is available to us if we just obey Him and walk by the word of His power. The psalmist reveals in Ps 119:2 (AMP), "Blessed (happy, fortunate, to be envied) are the undefiled (the upright, truly sincere, and blameless) in the way of the revealed will of God), who walk (order their conduct and conversation) in the law of the Lord (the whole of God's revealed will)."

God has given revelation knowledge to those who are upright in spirit and conversation. We are to lift up the name of Jesus in every conversation with the saved and the unsaved. God loves to see how we as believers conduct our affairs in the world. All eyes are on us because we are to be ambassadors of God, representatives of His saving grace. God's word is His divine revealed will. He wants us to worship Him wholeheartedly. When we give our all to Him, He makes us happy and gives us good fortune, so even our enemies will see the blessings on our lives.

Prayer: *Lord, help me to be obedient to Your will and Your way so that I may reap the benefits of Your righteous will. Enable me to walk upright before all men. Amen.*

CHAPTER 21: GOD IS OUR TRUST

Entrust your life, entrust your way of thinking, and entrust your plans to God for He is your provider and guide. God knows our ways, and He has given us freedom to make right decisions in life. It is up to us to seek His will for our lives before we inject our own will. We think that we are in charge of our own destiny, but God has been known to change circumstances to favor His agenda rather than our own plans or destiny that we see for ourselves.

God's agenda brings us to trust Him for everything, not just some things. Our desire should be to always ask, "What does God want for us? What is His assignment?" God will direct our paths if we allow Him to operate in His will for our lives. Sometimes, we want to take the lead for our own selfish reasons. God knows what's best for us, and He still allows us to make our own choices. He will reveal to us His destiny plans for us.

It is up to us to say, "Yes, Lord" or "No, Lord" to His plans. Look at the life of Moses. He was in the palace where God put Him. When it came to finding out of who he was, he could have received the hand of the princess, but Moses saw no shame in being the Hebrew that he was. He took on the identity that God gave Him rather than the identity that Pharaoh's daughter made for Him. He chose the path of faith and walked it with God. What path are you taking? The one God has given you, or the one you have decided to walk instead? (Proverbs 3:5-6).

Prayer: *Lord, help me to choose the right path, the one You have chosen for my life. I will trust Your plans for my future. Amen.*

CHAPTER 22: INTIMACY BY PRAYER

God hears our cries. He wants us to seek Him, call on Him, and tell Him about our problems and needs. God said He will hear us and give us peace. He will answer us according to His mercy. He will restore us to our rightful place in Him. God gives a promise and will keep it. He promised the children of Israel that after seventy years, the captivity in Egypt would end, and it did.

God is concerned about our welfare and peace. He is our hope and our great reward as we follow His teachings by faith. Many have cast down the word God put in their hearts, according to James 1:10. Satan always tries to turn you away from God's word. God's word works by the Law of Faith. The devil knows that once you believe that word in your heart, he has no control over your life. If Satan can't draw you away from the word of God, he has been defeated by you.

We pray honestly to God with our whole hearts daily. We allow that word to penetrate deep into our hearts and take root by faith. We can lean on God. Jeremiah 29:13 (AMP) states, "Then you will seek me, inquire for, and require me (as a vital necessity) and find me when you search for me with all your heart." We must hold fast to God's word, believe it, and allow our minds to be renewed by the washing of the word of God. Let us look at Hosea 4:6– "My people are destroyed for a lack of knowledge." Some Christians do not believe the entire Bible; they just want to accept parts of it.

We must believe God and trust Him. You must speak about what you want in prayer, believe what you need in prayer, claim what you have in Christ and keep faith and believe that you have received all by faith. The devil is a liar and a deceiver. Do not be fooled by Him.

***Prayer:** Lord, hear my prayers and take heed to my supplications. I am fully persuaded that I will have what I say and believe. Please keep me from doubt and unbelief. Amen.*

CHAPTER 23: TRUE REPENTANCE IS MINE

True repentance means many things. First of all, when you are sorry for anything you have done wrong and confess it in your spirit, you will have a release of heartfelt joy inside. Besides that, we must bring gifts fit for repentance. For example, if you are sorry about a wrong deed toward a fellow Christian, you must be willing to make recompense for that particular deed. If you took 500 dollars, you must pay back 500 dollars and then some if the person you wronged requires it. God wants to know that your heart is in the repentant state and that you are not just saying you are sorry with your lips. Many people may say they are sorry with their lips, but their hearts are still hardened against the person who was wronged them.

We as Christians are to follow after God, as the word proclaims in 1 John 2:12, "Therefore also now, saith the Lord, turn ye even to me with all your heart, and with fasting and with weeping, and with mourning." God wants us to be genuine with our repentance because He knows our hearts, and if our hearts deceive us, we may fall prey to the devil and his devices. We should not give the devil any room to enter into our lives, relationships, or daily living. He will use any deceitful way to come in when our words and ways do not line up with God's will for us. The Lord wants us to master any evil that comes our way. He wants us to be consecrated to Him and give ourselves to Him totally: body, mind, and spirit. We are to be obedient to the words of God, as Romans 12:21 (AMP) states, "Do not let yourself be overcome by evil but overcome (master) evil with good."

Prayer: *Thank You, Father, for hearing my groaning. I am genuinely brokenhearted for all my wrong thoughts and doings. Let Your faithful forgiveness rain down mercy from on high and restore a right spirit in me. Amen.*

CHAPTER 24: THE HOLY SPIRIT HELPS US TO PRAY

We have the help of the Holy Spirit when we pray sincerely from our hearts. The spirit of God helps us to make intercession because the Holy Spirit knows the mind of Christ. He makes supplication for us in such a way that God hears us and gives us His total attention.

Praying makes us joyful.

When we pray, we have the joy of the Lord that gives us strength in our spirit. Romans 8:27 states, "And he that searcheth the hearts knoweth the mind of the Spirit, because he maketh intercession for the saints according to the will of God."

When we seek the Lord, He gives us His strength. We will seek Him daily, as the word proclaims in Matthew 7:7, "Ask, and it shall be given you; seek and ye shall find; knock, and it shall be opened unto you."

God has made His divine word of His power available to us. He gives us the tools we need in order to have what we believe. You must believe before you can receive from God. Luke 18:1 states, "And he spake a parable unto them to this end: that men ought always to pray, and not to faint…"

There is a solemn call to all believers to pay attention to God's word. The word is a seed, and when it is planted in our hearts, it has to take root. If it does not take root, we have no power. The weak faint in times of adversity, but the strong keep standing until the results are given.

As children of the King, we have the ability to stand on the word, which is the final and solemn authority of God. Let's pay attention to Luke 21:36 (AMP): "Keep awake then and watch at all times [be discreet, attentive, and ready] praying that you may have the full strength and ability and be counted worthy to escape all these things [taken together] that will take place, and to stand in the presence of the Son of Man." God wants us to take a standby prayer to receive the strength that gives birth to His vision inside of us.

***Prayer:** Thank You, Father, for helping me to pray and stand on Your word. You increased my strength by the word of Your power. My heart rejoices in Your word. Thank You for hearing and answering my prayers. Amen.*

CHAPTER 25: GOD PROMISES TO ANSWER PRAYER

God has given us His word, and He will hear and answer our prayers. We must know all the benefits we have by our covenant blessings through Abraham. If we do not know our benefits, we will not take advantage of them. We need to be able to operate from a favorable position as kings and priests of The Most High. Prayer gets us to the door of faith, yet we must have the faith door key in order to unlock the provisions of God. God said in Isaiah 65:24, "And it shall come to pass that before they call, I will answer and while they are yet speaking, I will hear."

The Bible proclaims that we are the seeds of the blessed. Abraham was blessed to be a blessing, and his seeds were numbered as the sands of the sea. Surely, we are the seeds of Abraham. The same blessings and covenant promises we have received by God's grace. God will hear our cries and meet every need in our lives by His word. His word shall live for all eternity.

God has a remnant that He will bring through trials and tribulation. Zechariah 13:9 says, "And I will bring the third part through the fire, and will refine them as silver is refined and will try them as gold is tried; they shall call on my name, and I will hear them; I will say, 'It is my people,' and they shall say, 'the Lord is my God.'" God calls us out of the trials of a broken people. He wraps His arms of protection around us and holds us to His breast. Surely, He has proclaimed His inheritance for us and set in place a time of blessings and recompense.

He wants us to cling to Him, to abide in Him, and to ask for any and all things, as a child asks of a parent. He loves us, and He will fight for us. We belong to Him. Let us cry out to Him, as John 15:7 states, "If you abide in me, and my words abide in you, ye shall ask what ye will, and it shall be done unto you."

Prayer: *O' Lord of my salvation, I know You hear my call. I will call on You by faith, and You will hear me. I am Your child, and You are my Father and my Protector. Amen.*

CHAPTER 26: UNITED PRAYER

The term "corporate prayer" sounds like it is in reference to a business and all the people involved in it. Corporate prayer is, in fact, a total combination of all believers at a particular time praying in unison in one place and in one accord, petitioning and praising God at the same time. There is unity and power in prayer when all believers in one church or gathering bombard Heaven with thanksgiving, praise, and supplications, making our requests known unto God according to His word. God hears our cries and answers them all. In fact, Matthew 18:19 says, "Again I say unto you, that if two of you shall agree on Earth as touching anything that they shall ask, it shall be done for them of my father, which is in heaven."

We must believe what the Bible says and stand on it. When we do, we will receive a reward every time. God said it, and He is not a man that He should lie.

It is up to us to believe and trust God for every victory we obtain in this life. He said He would withhold no good thing from His children. You are God's child, and you know that He wants the best for you. He is waiting on you to claim the benefits of being His child. What if you had a long-lost uncle, and left you a million dollars in his will? You would not have a clue until someone informed you of the will. The word of God is God's will for us. We must read it to receive the revelation of His benefits for us. It doesn't matter who you are or what failures you may have come through. However unworthy you may feel, when you allow God to come into your heart, He makes you a new creation in Christ. We are made brand new to everything that is good and right for the first time.

Now, we want more of Him in our daily living. Prayer gets us to the throne of God, but faith and trust keep us there. God loves us unconditionally and takes pleasure in the prosperity of His people. When you pray, you prosper spiritually first. Seeking God is not for material things, but for the comfort of just being in His presence. Seeking God is not about possessions. It is about a renewed mind through Christ Jesus from the heart and the spirit. We have the mind of Christ that connects us to Him in a deeper relationship than ever before.

Do not be dismayed when God starts speaking to you in your spirit. When you start praying and meditating more and more on the word, this will inevitably happen.

Prayer: *Thank You, Father, for hearing my prayer. I come before You in the midst of many people. We cry out to You, and You hear us. Thank You for a renewed heart in the time of discouragement. Amen.*

CHAPTER 27: INTERCESSORY PRAYER

Out of deep concern and love, we want to pray for others, our sisters and brothers in Christ. We are knitted together by a common thread called love. Christ prayed for his disciples. Jesus prayed that his disciples would have perfect peace, confidence, coverage, comfort, and protection from the world. It gives me joy to know that Jesus has overcome the world and conquered for us. There is no need for distress, fear, or frustration about this physical world and its limitations. We are children of the Kingdom (God's way of doing things). We have the power and the authority to speak over a thing, and it shall manifest according to our faith. We are possessors of eternal life– the "Zoë" life– because the Anointed One lives inside of us.

Jesus prayed that we would receive eternal life in John 17:3 (AMP), as it states, "And this is eternal life: meaning to know [to perceive, recognize, become acquainted with, and understand] You, the only true and real God, and [likewise] to know Him, Jesus [as the Christ, the anointed one, the Messiah], whom You have sent. Jesus had an assignment to complete. He prayed for his disciples and all those who would follow them. What does this tell you about our work as believers? We are to pray for one another daily: our leaders, ministers, pastors, teachers, evangelists, and our government. We are to always pray and not to faint. God cannot have His perfect work performed in our lives when we allow these hindering spirits of confusion and strife to overtake our life of prayer, intercessory prayer for the brethren.

We are to be instruments of praise and worship given to the building up of God's covenant and house and the tearing down of Satan's house. God expects us to take a stand for righteousness and fight against the wiles of the devil.

Prayer: *Lord, help me to be an instrument of prayer for my fellow man and family. I want to restore the worst places in which Your people dwell and save wandering souls from destruction. Show me how to walk out this responsibility to the household of faith so that I may teach and save those who don't know the way. Amen.*

CHAPTER 28: THE CARNAL MIND

Unbelief started in the time of Moses when the children of Israel did not receive God's plan of deliverance. They continued murmuring against the man of God and complaining about their state, yet God was patient to all the children of Israel and continued to lead them toward the promised land. Moses was graced to do God's will.

God sent bread from Heaven, but they stated they didn't know what was sent when the small parcels appeared on the ground. Unbelief in a carnal mind can blind you to what is plainly revealed before your eyes. Although we have physical eyes that see, true understanding of God's ways and purpose have to be seen with spiritual eyes.

Just because you go to the house of prayer, it does not mean you are a prayerful person. We must examine ourselves fully so that we don't become carnal-minded (full of disobedience, unbelief, and selfishness) in the sight of God. God knows our hearts, and whatever is in the heart is what defines us. The scripture proclaims in Romans 8:7, "...the carnal mind is enmity against God: for it is not subject to the law of God, neither indeed can be." The carnal-minded man doesn't have any connection with God. He is not conscious of any of God's laws. They mean nothing to him; he couldn't care less. In fact, the carnal man is not bound or subject to the laws of God because he doesn't understand them. He totally rejects God's law, and he has never been born again.

The spiritual mind walks not with vanity, unbelief, and perverseness of spirit. The spirit-minded man or righteous man walks in the presence and guidance of the Holy Spirit. He knows who he is, and he is not intimidated by the devil. He is fully aware of the benefits and the provisions of God. He knows that God wants him to be blessed, and God takes pleasure in the prosperity of His people. We are God's people. Our minds are sound and full of knowledge and understanding. We are not as the unbelievers, those who are alienated, estranged and self-banished from God. We should walk with the knowledge of Romans 8:10, which states, "And if Christ be in you, the body is dead because of sin; but the Spirit is life because of righteousness."

Prayer: *Thank You, Father, for setting me free from the law of sin and death and giving me a mind and heart that please You by walking in Your blessed righteousness. Amen.*

CHAPTER 29: LET YOUR MIND BE UNDEFILED

Psalm 15:26 states, "The thoughts of the wicked are an abomination to the Lord, but the words of the pure are pleasant words."

When God is the center of your life, you know what to speak and decree. The Holy Spirit teaches you revelation knowledge of God's advantages and how this world system works. We are not alone; we have the guidance and comfort of the Holy Ghost forever. We must allow Him to govern and rule on our behalf. He speaks to us out of the abundance of God's word planted on the depths of our hearts. Let us look at the words of Proverbs 23:7, as it states, "For as he thinketh in his heart, so is he…"

We have to be careful and conscious of the words we speak. We need only to speak victory, not calamity on ourselves or others. We are not blinded by the wiles and schemes of the devil. He tried to deceive Christ, the Son of God. He will use every evil device he can to get you to say the wrong thing, especially words of doubt.

Think about the story of Esau. He cared little about his birthright. He allowed the devil to operate through his words when he said, "What good is it if I'm hungry?" The hunger was temporary, yet Esau spoke against his birthright just to receive a bowl of lentils. It doesn't take a rocket scientist to figure out that just because you're hungry right now, it doesn't mean you won't eat at another hour. Esau just didn't respect the promise. He didn't care what happened at that moment. He didn't give it a second thought. His attitude found him out by the words he spoke of his own choosing. We must be cautious at all times about what our hearts release into the atmosphere when we speak without the spirit of God's counsel.

If we make a mistake, let us repent quickly before God. The word reveals to us in Titus 1:15-16, "Unto the pure all things are pure: but unto them that are defiled and unbelieving is nothing pure; but even their mind and conscious is defiled."

The word "defiled" means that there is nothing in that person's understanding of what is right to prevent them from doing wrong. When one's conscious is defiled, there is no revelation knowledge about the ways and benefits of God. Only one's selfish will is what matters in the present and the future. There is no sorrow or repentance of any wrongdoings.

Prayer: *Father, I thank You for a pure conscious and the love of justice that You have put on the inside of my unconscious heart and mind so that I may be led by Your Holy Spirit. Amen.*

CHAPTER 30: WHAT MAKES YOUR THOUGHTS EVIL?

Our words determine our destiny. An answer from one's mouth can influence the behavior of others. We as Christians have to be joyful and operate out of love and a pure heart toward our fellow man. Proverbs 15:26 states, "The thoughts of the wicked are an abomination to the Lord: but the words of the pure are pleasant words." The Lord wants us to think before we answer. We are to determine and discern what to speak. A righteous person has a path to travel that the Holy Spirit makes clear. We are going higher to the greater revelations and moves of God. We exercise grace, knowing that all issues flow from what dwells on the inside. The Bible tells us that our thinking resonates from the heart. Pressure, concern, peace, and even the comfort all come from the heart. You must guard your heart so that you do no evil or sin against God. The heart is where the word of God takes root.

If we seek after the things of God that bring peace, not folly, we do well. The scripture says in Proverbs 23:7, "For as he thinketh in his heart, so is he." The Lord sees us as children; as a child grows, he become familiar with the routine of discipline. When he cries, his parents may respond quickly. If the child asks for something verbally, his parents may not respond as quickly. We don't have to worry about our Heavenly Father responding to us quickly. He hears every cry and call from His children. He loves us in spite of our shortcomings and imperfections.

Know the path that you take. Be watchful because the evil one comes at the weakest points of our lives. Be not a friend with the world, for he who is a friend with the world is an enemy to God. Trust God to provide all you need, and He will add no sorrow with it.

Prayer: *Thank You, Father, for keeping my thoughts and teaching me to know my heart and the ways of wicked men so that I can discern Your guidance and not stumble. Amen.*

CHAPTER 31: THE LORD KNOWS OUR THOUGHTS

God knows the intent of our hearts. He made us in His image. Therefore, we are known of Him. We as spirit-filled believers are to be like Jesus. We are to be discerners of the hearts and minds of people as the power of God's love abides in us. The Holy Spirit will speak to us and reveal the secrets of people's hearts.

Many events took place during Jesus' ministry. He felt the resistance of so many naysayers and unbelievers that he spoke to, yet he spoke to them concerning the condition of their hearts. Their wicked hearts were so strong. Jesus felt it in his spirit all the time. The scripture reveals to us in Matthew 9:4, "And Jesus knowing their thoughts said, Wherefore think ye evil in your hearts?" Jesus could so easily discern the evil in their hearts from their thoughts.

Jesus caused a man with palsy to be healed by saying, "Your sins be forgiven you", but the scribes were offended and called him a blasphemer, not knowing he had the power to make the man whole in body and spirit. Many people confuse wholeness with the ability to be perfect in body and strength. It was not just the physical body made whole, but he was made whole. The man was healed; he was healed physically and spiritually. God even heals your relationships, business affairs, position finances, and your mind.

We need to stop putting limits on God and allow the Holy Spirit to operate in our lives fully and liberally. Many people cry out to God to help them in times of trouble and trials, but as soon as the need is met or their bodies are healed, some become high-minded, unfaithful, and vain in their thoughts because they are void of understanding about the source of their provision or healing. They take for granted the blessings and the Provider of those blessings.

What has deceived you? What has darkened your mind or imagination into thinking you will not need God again? There is a veil of deception there, and it separates us from God. God may decide to take the blessings away, yet He gives gifts without repentance. God will always rescue us from ourselves.

Why go into bondage again and be deceived by the wicked one? He doesn't care about you. Don't let fear and guilt come in and choke the word. Those who allow that to happen start to believe they are missing something that God has not provided for them. They are blinded because they don't listen to God's truth; they prefer to go their own way. We must be able to hear the voice of God and resist the voice of the devil and know the difference. God's voice will refer back to His word. In fact, His voice confirms His word.

> ***Prayer:*** *Thank You, Father, for helping me to have good thoughts and a right mind to call on You and stay in the word day and night. Amen.*

CHAPTER 32: WE POSSESS SPIRITUAL MINDS

Romans 8:6 states, "For to be carnally minded is death; but to be spiritually minded is life and peace." When we have the spirit of God in us, we can please Him. Having a spiritual mind makes us obedient to God. We have become new creatures in Christ. We obtain a fresh anointing that enables us to do righteous things that are pleasing to God.

We now have the Holy Spirit and the word of God working on the inside of us. By the Holy Spirit, we are quickened to understand revelation knowledge. God has given us grace to become ministers of the new covenant, knowing that all blessings flow from the covenant inheritance we have through Christ Jesus. As we are inspired by the scriptures daily, we are reminded in 2 Corinthians 3:6, "That God has made us able ministers of the new testament; not of the letter, but of the spirit: for the letter killeth, but the spirit giveth life."

Through Christ, God has written us a letter of the heart and not of stone and has taken all condemnation from us so that we may be righteous vessels whereby His spirit may dwell with us in peace. God has written

His laws in our hearts, not to force us to become doers of the word but so that we will love the word and do it because we have the heart of God living in us.

We have confidence in God, knowing that He will supply all our needs and provide all sufficiency to carry out His will by His covenant of righteousness– not our own righteousness, but His righteousness– dwelling on the inside of us. As the word reveals to us in 2 Corinthians 3:17, "Now the Lord is that Spirit: and where the Spirit of the Lord is, there is liberty." In Christ, our spiritual hope, we have boldness, and we speak that we know of him from our hearts for our minds are enlightened by him.

Prayer: *Thank You, Father, for life and a spiritual mind that enables me to live in the fullness of Your grace and power for I have confidence in You, and I trust You. Amen.*

CHAPTER 33: WE HAVE THE MIND OF CHRIST

God has given us the ability to hear Him. We are children of the most high and have an advocate in the Holy Ghost. He is our Pathfinder, our Teacher, and our Guide into all of God's divine knowledge and wisdom. God gives us counsel concerning our lives, our circumstances, and the purpose God has chosen for our lives. We are to know the desires of God's heart, and if we don't know them, we must get busy in finding out what they are through His word.

Corinthians 2:16 (AMP) states, "For who has known or understood the mind (the counsels and purposes) of the Lord so as to guide and instruct him and give him knowledge? But we have the mind of Christ (the Messiah) and do hold the thoughts (feelings and purposes) of his heart."

The mind of Christ gives us the authority and power to walk in victory to carry out God's mission. He has placed His vision and purpose down on the inside of our hearts. He will fulfill them and bring them to fruition in His time.

The heart of God is revealed to us in His word. His precepts give us all we need to discern what is good, proper, and necessary to be obedient to God's word. He equips us for every assignment, and He gives us the provisions to perform them. We have all sufficiency to do every good work speedily. The temple of God dwells on the inside of us along with the spirit of God, who directs our paths. 1 Corinthians 3:16 states, "We are a holy temple set apart to do the work of our Father."

We are the masterpiece of God. He designed us for His pleasures to do His work. We are to walk by faith and do the work of a good soldier willingly forever. God will be with you and keep you from all hurt harm and danger. He knows the deeds of the wicked and will deal with them in accordance with their selfish acts. We are to demonstrate the love of God toward our fellow man. We are not to be unjust in helping those who have lost hope or become victims of the evil one. We must be merciful to those who feel hopeless. Our lives may be the only Bible some may read in life. Our destiny is to be the ambassadors for Christ. God has a plan for our lives. Listen to what His love tells us in Jeremiah 29:11– "For I know the thoughts that I think toward you, saith the Lord, thoughts of peace, and not of evil, to give you an expected end."

Prayer: *Thank You, Father, for the mind of Christ. Thank You for equipping me with the power to get results by Your Holy Spirit. Amen.*

CHAPTER 34: BE AN EXAMPLE AS CHRIST JESUS

We need the develop the attitude of a humble spirit. God gives us wisdom and understanding. We cannot do anything of ourselves. God's super with our natural enables us to do miraculous things. God wants us to have an attitude of humility. We don't have to boast or prove anything to the world. All we have to do is to let God take control of our hearts and souls. Jesus, being the son of God, didn't think that he was above obeying the Father. He was meek and lowly in all his teachings and doings.

He always spoke of the Father giving him the power and the authority to do great works. He never took credit for anything the Father enabled him to do. He prayed and gave God the honor for performing miracles in the crowds. He said, "I do what my Father tells me to do." Philippians 2:5-6 (AMP) states, "Have this same attitude in yourselves which was in Christ Jesus [look to him as your example in selfless humility], who, although He existed in the form and unchanging essence of God [as One with Him, possessing the fullness of all the divine attributes – the entire nature of deity], did not regard equality with God a thing to be grasped or asserted…"

Christ knew his clear purpose, and he was not distracted by the cunning or deceptive ways of man or the devil. He knew his assignment and even the time of its end. Imagine having to endure the horrors of knowing how your life will end and the things you will have to endure, yet you do it with joy, despising the shame. Jesus never turned to the right hand nor to the left hand. He moved straight on to his calling with an attitude of gratefulness.

He was grateful that the Father had chosen him for such a task. He is that lamb who was born from the foundation of the world. He had a divine assignment to fulfill, and he did it well and with joy. Let us adopt this same attitude of gratefulness and joy as we walk in the master plan God has chosen for our lives in such a time as this.

Prayer: *Father, give me strength to endure the task and walk in my calling so that I may do Your will with exceeding gratefulness and joy. Amen.*

CHAPTER 35: THINKING SOBERLY BY FAITH

The Lord wants us to redeem the times and take notice at our lives. We are so concerned about what other people think of us. We are busy trying to look like the latest movie star. Are we not to please God and do His will, being renewed in our spirits and minds? We should not think of ourselves more highly than we ought. We cannot become selfish because whatever comes out of selfishness is evil. God has given us a measure of faith that is able to make us wise in the things of God. We all make up one body, but God has given us many gifts that can enhance the church body and save the souls of many who are weak in this world. God's grace is sufficient, but we must be obedient to the word, cheerful in our giving, and we must love our neighbor as ourselves.

The children of God must be sober-minded and upright in character. Romans 12:3 (AMP) states, "For by the grace [of God] given to me I say to everyone of you not to think more highly of himself [and of his importance and ability] than he ought to think; but to think so as to have sound judgment, as God has apportioned to each a degree of faith [and a purpose designed for service]". It is our God-given duty to walk in humility, be wise, and be conscious of the need for others to unite with us to bring about the purpose of our destiny on Earth and live up to God's expectations of us. He gives us grace and mercy because none are perfect; only He is faithful and just.

The word states that we must wait on our ministering or teaching, as described in Romans 12:7. God is the one who exalted us and gives us the ability to do all good works with diligence and cheerfulness. We are to honor one another, love all men equally without dissimulation, and abhor that which is evil for God knows our hearts, and the candle of our spirit is lit before Him for all eternity. Let us walk upright before God and man so that God may honor us with exhortations in due time.

Prayer: *Thank You, Father, for helping me to think soberly by faith, trusting You for every act of mercy and kindness so that I may be worthy of Your grace, wisdom, and exhortation. Amen.*

CHAPTER 36: THINK ON THE THINGS THAT BRING PEACE

Many Christians think or meditate on things that are negative. If you meditate on the negative, you will get the same result as if you were meditating on the positive. The scriptures tell us to think on those things that are true. The word of God is true. The Lord said seek the truth and the truth will make you free. We are not free to enjoy the benefits of being children of God if we are not living and speaking the truth, which is the word of God. God wants us to have peace of mind and spirit so that we are able to discern what is right and resist evil.

God wants us to have the ability to make sound decisions, walk in love and love justice. It is time to be honest with yourself and God. The time for pretending is over because God knows our hearts. We need to pray mightily and be thankful for all that God has done, and if He doesn't do another thing for us, He has already done more than enough. Meditate on these things, as Philippians 4:8 states, "Finally, brethren, whatsoever things are true, whatsoever things are honest, whatsoever things are just, whatsoever things are pure, whatsoever things are lovely, whatsoever things are of good report; if there be any virtue, and if there be any praise, think on these things."

The Holy Spirit has taught us to keep these precepts as we grow in grace and anointing. Anointing coincides with all the methods that bring about true Christianity. We are in love with God and His statutes. In order to have all that God wants for us and walk in the fullness of His knowledge, we must think on these things and not waiver. Surely, these are the positive things that bring about true riches and abundant life that God wants us to live.

He has promised to keep in perfect peace those whose minds are stayed on Jesus. We must be in right standing with God to receive all the benefits of sonship.

Prayer: *Lord, thank You for Your direction and for keeping my mind in perfect peace so that I can meditate on the true, just, and pure wisdom of Your word. Amen.*

CHAPTER 37: CONSIDER GOD'S PROVISIONS

God wants us to consider our ways. Our ways should line up with His ways, but sometimes we don't really understand who God is. We must believe that He is a rewarder of those who seek Him. Let's consider God's purpose for giving us clear direction and discipline. He chastises and disciplines us because He loves us. You want your child to be the best at all his endeavors and ultimately succeed. God wants the same for us. He wants us to avoid the pitfalls of our mistakes, and He doesn't want us to dwell on the past. He wants us to get rid of guilt and despair about little things and get on with the big picture of our lives. We are His disciples, led and taught by Him. We are the offspring of past generations, and He keeps blessing us at different levels of our lives.

God has been so good and done so many great things for us. We are grateful. God is Creator and Architect of the universe. He has made the moon, the stars, the rivers, and all creeping things. He has put everything in its place and the waters at their boundaries. The psalmist in Psalm 8:4 says, "What is man that thou art mindful of him? And the son of man, that Thou visited him?" God made man a little lower than the angels, and He loved us. He made us in His own image with the dust from the earth.

Everything else was spoken into existence, but God took the time to mold and shape man into His own likeness. What an honor for us by the hand and power of God.

We have disappointed God with our dealings in the world. We have much, but we are never satisfied. We drink and eat, yet it's never enough. He clothes us, yet we say we are not warm. We're always wanting and needing something more than what we have and finding ourselves with no contentment. God is forever blessing us with His abundant life. He takes care of us, even the lilies of the fields. Let us consider that He is ready to meet every need. As the scripture says in Matthew 6:29, He feeds the birds and clothes the lilies, yet Solomon in all his glory was not arrayed as one of these.

Prayer: *Father, thank You for all the comfort and provisions You have given and the matchless blessings of hope and love. I will consider all Your wonderful works and marvel in them. Amen.*

CHAPTER 38: THE CHARACTERISTICS OF THE SPIRITUAL MIND

A child of God is always prepared to do the will of God. Are you prepared? Many believers don't want to read the word of God or even listen to any word of God outside of Sunday worship. When we go to God's house on Sunday, we are to worship Him totally, which is good. Nevertheless, we must listen to the voice of God and our Teacher, the Holy Ghost, so that we may be able to endure life's challenges throughout the days and months.

The word of God blesses us and encourages us to stir up the gifts and abilities that God puts inside us. God wants us to be spiritually, mentally, and physically prepared for His battles. We are warriors fighting for justice because God is just. God wants us to have rest from our works. We rest in His word by refreshing our spirits anew every morning. We have entitlements and blessings; therefore, we need to be strong physically to go in to claim the land, build, take over, and occupy blessings, as well as help the poor and needy and provide for our families. We know that God is with us, but we cannot do anything without the guidance of the word constantly in front of our eyes, in our ears, and in our mouths. God tells us in Joshua 1:8, "This book of the law shall not depart out of thy mouth; but thou shalt meditate therein day and night, that thou mayest observe to do according to all that is written therein; for thou shall make thy way prosperous, and then thou shalt have good success." God wants us to be doers of the word and not hearers only. He expects great things from us because He blesses us all the time. God has left a road map for us to follow, and it is written so plain, a fool need not error. He tells us what will bring us success and a favorable outcome of all our understanding and knowledge of Him. We shall be prosperous if we endure life like good soldiers, keeping our minds on His word and His precepts.

Doing things God's way will get us the outcome we desire. He has set His laws to bring life more abundantly to all His children, and we truly can call Him Abba Father because He is the best Father there will ever be.

Prayer: *Thank You, Father, for Your words of life that will keep me in health and prosperity. I will meditate on Your words day and night and do them well. Amen.*

CHAPTER 39: GOD SETS US APART FOR HIMSELF

God wants us to be totally subject to His direction and lean neither on our own hearts nor our own understanding. Why? Because God knows how we are wired. The issues of life come from the heart of man, and we must be confident and trust God to give us right discernment. Our thoughts must line up with His words. He promises to keep in perfect peace those whose minds are stayed on Him. Let us revere God and be still in His rest so that we sin not. Let us hide His word in our hearts so that we will sin not against Him.

God will give us divine favor as we keep still and allow our thoughts to receive the insight and revelation of His divine care. Proverbs 3:4 states, "So shalt thou find favor and good understanding in the sight of God and man." God wants us to listen to the prophet that God has entrusted us to for guidance. We will be able to grow from faith to faith and glory to glory. He will establish us, so shall we prosper. He assures our success by depending on Him, as detailed in 2 Chronicles 20:20. We think that doing the work of God is just going to church, singing songs, and dancing in the aisles. God's love and blessings for us do not stop at the prayer house or on our knees.

The word of God, specifically Psalm 4:4-5 (AMP), states, "Tremble [with anger or fear], and do not sin; Meditate in your heart upon your bed and be still [reflect on your sin and repent of your rebellion]. Selah. Offer righteous sacrifices; Trust [confidently] in the Lord."

God wants us to meditate in our hearts to examine our own spirits and offer sacrifices worthy of His acceptance that we be not puffed up in pride and get His mercy. We must remember the pit that He brought us out of and of which we could not get ourselves out. We depend on Him, and He shows up and delivers us from all snares of unrighteousness. He keeps us in right standing with Him so that we may see the good He has bestowed upon us in spite of our disobedience and frailty of heart and mind. He put gladness in our hearts and gave us the oil of joy so that we may dwell in peace and safety forever.

Prayer: *Father, thank You for setting us apart in our hearts so that we sin not. We put all our trust in You for You give us peace and make us dwell in safety forever and ever. Amen.*

CHAPTER 40: LET MY MEDITATION BE ACCEPTABLE TO GOD

God is our refuge and shield. He is the rock of our salvation. He wants us to use our gifts to rightly divide the word of truth. In order to tap into God's perfect will, we must practice being in His presence. What I mean by that is we must allow the meditation on God's word and His goodness to penetrate the very depths of our souls and beings. The Lord is our rock and our Redeemer, according to Psalm 19:14. God is our strength; we don't need any false stimuli to get us to understanding that we are speaking spirits. We have the anointing of the Holy Spirit to usher in the supernatural so that it can reside with the natural. All we have to do is speak it and believe it, and God shall bring it to pass.

We are strengthened in the Lord by treating our brothers and sisters and all strangers with respect. We must cultivate the gifts that God has given us or we'll become idle, not following the guidance of the Holy Ghost and the word of God, which are able to make us strong in grace.

Everything we do and say must be acceptable to God. He wants us to operate in His wisdom, doing those things that are beneficial to all believers. He wants us to rely on His word and walk upright before all so that our profiting may be seen by all men.

God wants us to teach and minister His word in total truth. 1 Timothy 4:12 states, "Let no man despise thy youth; but be thou an example of the believers, in word, in conservation, in charity, in spirit, in faith, impurity."

We are to study the word of God and be able to talk about it to others, as well as minister the word by the Holy Spirit and love one another.

Our faith must be strong, and we must give exhortation to the teachings and statutes so that we are able to make us wise in doing, giving, and edifying the body of Christ Jesus. You must do those things that God wants and likes for you are the apple of His eye.

Prayer: *Thank You, God, for the exhortation of Your word in power and in truth so that we may be examples to all believers in word, charity, conversation, and faith. Amen.*

CHAPTER 41: THINKING, QUIETNESS, AND CALMNESS

God puts us in quiet habitation that assures you that no fear or evil can stand in your way. Are you upset and easily disquieted in your spirit? God gives us a special place of comfort that renews us day by day. Isaiah 32:17 states, "And the work of righteousness shall be peace; and the effect of righteousness, quietness and assurance forever." We know that the presence of God in our hearts and minds is crucial. Without the presence of God in our hearts, we cannot function as sound-minded Christians. Joy is our way to overcome any circumstance. We can fight the good fight of faith by resting in the joy of the Lord. God wants us to have peace in our lives.

Many Christians have strife and confusion about life's circumstances, but God gives us victory and quietness over everything we face in this world. We are not of the world, even if we are in the world. We are commanded to study, work with our hands, and mind our business. In order to receive the quiet stillness of God's presence, we must do as the word of God reveals to us by the Holy Spirit. We must follow His word. 1 Thessalonians 4:11 states, "And that ye study to be quiet, and to do your own business, and to work with your own hands, as we commanded you."

In order to have a quiet and still life, we must be obedient to the word of God. If we do those things that are right and good, God will take care of every one of our needs and concerns. He keeps us as a father keeps his child and as a mother takes away the nipple so that the child may not want the nipple but will see that he needs the bottle so that he can be all that he needs to be to grow and flourish as a person.

We are to be whole before God. God's wholeness means that nothing is broken or missing. Our lives are modeled and given over to the righteousness of our Lord and savior Jesus Christ.

Prayer: *Thank You, Lord, for quieting my spirit and keeping me in Your presence. I love You, Lord. I am made to study, to be quiet, and to rest in Your commandments. Amen.*

CHAPTER 42: REST IN THE LORD

Only the divine presence of God can give you rest. God promises to give rest to our bodies, souls, and spirits. Many people feel that resting from their labors and work in a secular job define this rest. This rest is a rest that can only come from God in every area of your life. Psalm 23:3 (AMP) states, "He refreshes and restores my soul (life); He leads me in the paths of righteousness for His name's sake."

God keeps me in right standing with Him because I seek Him early in prayer. I commune with Him about all my life victories and failures. He causes me to lie down in peace. He protects me wherever I go. He provides good things in a quiet and calm habitation. I will praise Him for all the days of my life. Lift up your voice and lift up your head to Almighty God for He is an awesome God. His paths are full of joy, love, blessings, and prosperity. He even gives us the desires of our hearts.

No matter what stumbling blocks the devil tries to put in your way, just look over your life and see where God has brought you from. Speak about the blessings and think about the victories and dark places God has brought you through. He will keep on doing good things for you. He has opened doors that were shut to me. He has put me in high positions that I thought I could not handle; hence, He provided a way for me to understand it all. Sometimes, we lose the "rest" of God when we step out of His will. You have to decide in your own heart and mind to follow God's destiny for your life. Don't lose sight of His perfect will or fall into disobedience and refuse to hear the voice of God calling you by faith and divine revelation. We must hear His voice, or we will not receive His anointing, the divine enabling that brings us closer to our creator.

***Prayer:** Thank You, Father, for allowing me to receive Your rest: rest for my body, mind, soul, and spirit. I will walk in Your provisions so that I may receive rest forever more. Amen.*

CHAPTER 43: MEDITATION IN SILENCE

It is good to be watchful over our tongue. People tend to say a lot of words, yet those words carry little meaning to helping their situation or honoring God. It is an honorable thing to keep silent when all hell is breaking loose, and we have confidence in God and how He is handling our situation. We can be sure that everything will be all right.

When your enemies are plotting against you, keep silent and let God fight the battles. He will give you strategies to keep on enacting the plan He has laid out for you, so there is no stopping, but blessings continue to flow. Many people cares about work, making deals, increasing their positions, and accumulating worldly things. God is telling us to count those things as nothing and vain because we know not who those things will belong to after we are gone. As detailed in Psalm 39:6), our hope is to be in God, and we should follow His way of doing things, His plan, and His wonderful love for us all.

He wants us to walk in that pure love and life that has no end or limits. We can ask what we will, and it shall be given by our Abba Father. We have to practice patience and silence in order for God to do His perfect work on us and through us. It's not enough to have all the blessings and anointing put on us but never allow for God's power to flow through us. Look at the psalmist's plea to God in Psalm 39:8– "Deliver me from all my transgressions; make me not the reproach of the foolish."

God wants to use our lives and citizenship in His Kingdom so that we may be able to bring others in and they can see God's hand on our lives and go after those ways in Christ. This is how the covenant operates in such a time as this. Many people don't know how wonderfully blessed they are. We can show them that they don't have to fight their own battles. God will fight for us. God will give us recompense for all the devil has ever stolen from us. God has lifted up a standard against the devil and his demonic hosts. God will not stand by and allow his people to live in poverty. His blessings cover us.

***Prayer:** Thank You, God, for the power You give us to hold our peace before our adversaries and receive demonstration of Your power and remain in confidence that all is well in our lives. Amen.*

CHAPTER 44: SPEAKING WISDOM WITH AN EXCELLENT SPIRIT

To tame the tongue is the plight of wise men. We as Christians have a ridiculously hard time with taming our tongues. We carelessly say the wrong things at the wrong times. In order to bring contentment to our lives, we must know how to communicate to all men with sound speech. The Bible tells us, "He that hath knowledge sparest his words; and a man of understanding is of an excellent spirit" (Proverbs 17:27). That excellence is a spirit of calmness and coolness that rests on a child of God who has confidence in God's plans and trusts God to bring them to pass.

The just walk by faith, not by sight. God has not given us a spirit of fear but of love, power, and a sound mind (2 Timothy 1:7). We have minds of understanding. We have the mind of Christ; therefore, we operate by the authority that God has given us by the Holy Spirit. He guides us in the direction of peace and strategies to solve any problem. He shows us where to turn and follow. He gives us witty inventions and creative wisdom to do all that is assigned to us.

Some Christians become bitter in their communication because certain trials and actions of others may cause some discomfort to the flesh and the emotions, and then they become offended. God wants us to be champions of grace and sound communicators to all people. Words can make or break your deliverance. You have to speak good things over your life even when you don't see that much favor.

God has a process He takes us through, but we have to be ready to endure that process He takes us through. We must give it all we've got to endure the light afflictions, so we can reap a far greater reward if we faint not. When things get tough, it shows God what we're made of. The word shows us in 2 Timothy 1:13 (AMP) that we must purpose in our hearts to "hold fast and follow the pattern of wholesome and sound teaching which you have heard from me, in (all) the faith and love which are (for us) in Christ Jesus."

We must follow sound teaching, as Paul told Timothy, because it is Jesus Christ who gives us the love and soundness of spirit. God loved us enough to pour the love of Jesus into us when we were yet sinners.

Prayer: *Thank You, God, for a sound mind and sound teaching that enable me to embrace Your love, so I can love others by my speaking, living, and giving. Amen.*

CHAPTER 45: OUR WORDS HAVE POWER

God's word reveals to us that what we say determines our outcome. We as Christians must be alert to the fact that we can speak negatively or positively in our lives and the lives of others. In our tongue rests the ability to fail or succeed in every area of our lives. Consider James 3:2 (AMP): "For we all stumble and sin in many ways. If anyone does not stumble in what he says [never saying the wrong thing], he is a perfect man [fully developed in character, without serious flaws], able to bridle his whole body and rein in his entire nature [taming his human faults and weaknesses]". We are responsible for our standing with God. Faith is what moves God, not crying, yelling, sweating, or begging. God responds to faith. If you have the confidence that your faith is strong and immovable and stand on that conviction that God has what you need and will supply all your needs according to His riches in glory through Christ Jesus, stand firm in that confession. God will have to show up. Sometimes we give up to soon. We start hitting and missing if we try to figure out when and how God will bless us or do the thing we asked for. All we have to do is trust Him and keep still. Surely, we can pray, but don't pray the problem. We are to pray the solution, the answer to the problem. Start thanking God for the victory before you can see it manifest in the natural. We are creatures of faith, and with what God says in His promises, we are totally persuaded that He will perform His word.

Those who possess the wisdom of God are instructed by the Holy Spirit; therefore, they speak with understanding and persuasiveness to convince all that are in oppression and experience heaviness of heart. To speak words of encouragement and pleasantness gives the hearers strength and enables others to become strengthened in spirit, mind, and body. Proverbs 16:24 (AMP) states, "Pleasant words are as a honeycomb, sweet to the mind and healing to the body."

***Prayer:** Father, thank You for giving me the power to speak strength, health, and prosperity into the lives of Your people. Let the words of my mouth continue to build up Your people into wholeness by Your divine covenant. Amen.*

CHAPTER 46: SEVEN STEPS TO TRANSFORM YOUR THINKING

As detailed in Romans 12:1-3, we the children of God are to be transformed into His way of thinking and His way of doing things. The transformation of the mind has to be processed by our resistance to the world's way of thinking and doing things. The question that has to be asked is "How do you change a man?" The answer is by changing his way of thinking. We as children of the Most High have to understand all the concepts that apply to this transformation process, according to the word of God. They are given in seven steps, as follows:

Step One: Present Your Body As A Living Sacrifice

As detailed in 1 Peter 4:2, we are no longer to live our days in subject to the flesh or to the lust of men, but to the will of God. We must ask God what it is that He wants us to do. We are to be examples of a care-free lifestyle, in which we exhibit total commitment to do the work God has called us to do. How do we find out what that work is? We simply need to go to God in prayer and meditate on His word, and He will speak to us and reveal what His will is. Many people don't have a clue about their destiny or what the plan of God is for their lives. We should be able to hear God's voice clearly. You can hear

His voice behind the sermons preached or even hear His voice from meditating on the word day and night.

We are to become disciples of God, forsaking our own personal agenda and desires but allowing the Holy Spirit to wash us with the word, renewing our mind daily. We think about possessions too much, and we think about decorating, and we think about buying the latest vehicle. Let us show God that our focus can be on Him, and He will provide all our needs and fulfill our desires. God confirms His promises to us, and He keeps His word. He is not a man that he should lie (Numbers 23:19). The scripture tells us in Luke 18:29-30, "And he said unto them, Verily I say unto you, There is no man that hath left house, or parents, or brethren, or wife, or children, for the kingdom of God's sake, Who shall not receive manifold more in this present time, and in the world to come life everlasting." We have God's guarantee to bless us more than we can hope for in this lifetime. His word has promised it.

Prayer: Thank You, Father, for accepting me. I give my body as a living sacrifice to serve You and to do Your work here in Your church by the power of Your word by Christ Jesus. Amen.

Step Two: Be Not Conformed To This World

To be conformed means to accept the ways and governing laws of a system. We are citizens of God's Kingdom system. We are not out of the world yet, but we don't have to do things the way the world does them. This world system is not designed to solve your problems or to get you out of debt. This world is designed by men and women who want everything by toiling and fighting against one another. God tells us in His word that if we ask in the name of Jesus Christ, we shall receive. We must trust God and believe that He will perform all that He promised. His word does not come back void, and He is not a man that He should lie. What's in this world causing you to conform to it? Are you not in the knowledge and wisdom of God? The Bible tells us that we are to be lenders, not the borrowers. We should be the distributors to all those who have mental, physical, and spiritual needs. God expects us to be a light unto the world. We are to build the waste places and operate in authority as ambassadors for Christ. The Bible tells of many people who were transformed by the word of God. They began to think like Jesus because they were filled with anointing.

Peter, the cursing fisherman, becomes a man whose very shadow heals people, according to Matthew 26:74). The woman of Samaria with a vile reputation becomes an evangelist of truth (John 4:17-18). Saul, the violent persecutor, becomes Paul, the tender-hearted brother (Acts 9:1).

Just think about the way you were a few years ago. Think about how Jesus transformed your heart and changed your mind through the power of the word and God's saving grace. We didn't deserve it, and we didn't earn it. It was a gift given by the love of our Heavenly Father. He met us just where we were and gave us "shalom".

Prayer: *Father, thank You for transforming my life. Thank You for believing in me even though I was a sinner without hope and full of despair. You renewed my mind and put in me a new spirit. Amen.*

Step Three: Be Holy And Acceptable To God, Which Is Your Reasonable Service

To be holy is to be set apart, doing those things that are pleasing to God. We are led by the spirit of God, and we hear God's voice. We have an earnest relationship with God when we realize who He is. We cannot treat God as holy if we can't identify ourselves as holy, even when we have some faults.

Our ability to be holy comes from God's acceptance of Jesus' sacrifice on the cross. When we accept Jesus as our personal savior, we become righteous by the righteousness of Jesus Christ that is given to us, and we take on those same characteristics as Jesus himself.

We are commanded to be holy or we will not see Jesus, and we will not have a deep relationship with him. We become blind to our own selfish needs and desires when we accept holy disconnection from the world's way of doing things. We see the importance of this in 2 Peter 3:11, as it says, "Seeing then that all these things shall be dissolved, what manner of person ought ye to be in all holy conversation and godliness." It is not enough to call yourself a Christian and not walk or live by example with Christ as your guide.

This world's means, pleasures, and things to be desired are temporal. The only true riches and possessions are those that are not tangible. A true relationship with Jesus Christ outweighs all these possessions.

Our conversation should be that of faith, seasoned with reverence and love toward all people. You are to walk in obedience to God's commands at every level of faith. We are to be prepared and ready to conduct ourselves in a holy manner in deed and conversation. Holiness is not something supernatural; it is how God expects us to live until His coming. This is a daily, consistent walk of faith that has to be nurtured and practiced until Jesus comes.

Don't think because this word "holy" seems so powerful and dramatic, only a select few can live it and the rest of us have to just throw up our hands and say, "I can't do it."

Holy living is living in peace and brotherly love, walking blamelessly, owing no man in deed, operating in readiness by studying the word and receiving the revelation from it, staying in prayer and worship, and doing unto others as you would have them to do unto you. God wants steadfastness and for you to resist the devil's impulses.

Prayer: *Thank You, Father, for giving me the confidence, renewed faith, and strength to serve my fellow man so that I may serve You in all that You have assigned for me to do in this life cycle. Amen.*

Step Four: Be Ye Transformed By The Renewing Of Your Mind

God wants us as believers to surrender to Him totally: mind, body and spirit. He wants us to be consecrated to the renewing of ourselves from the natural and crucify the flesh. Therefore, we must renew the mind and separate it from this world system so that we may know true holiness. The transition from worldliness to holiness takes a spiritual renewal of the mind by the word.

The enlightenment God gives His people brings revelation to all areas of our lives. Look at 2 Corinthians 4:6 –"For God, who commanded the light to shine out of darkness, hath shined in our hearts, to give the light of the knowledge of the glory of God in the face of Jesus Christ." The light of God's word is given to us, but it is manifested by the grace of Christ Jesus. Without the love of God abiding in you, you are totally without His revelation.

Revelation is the key to finding the fullness of God in order to obtain "power" for we are weak if we have not the power of God. Let us look at 2 Corinthians 4:7. It gives us that confirmation, as it says, "But we have this treasure in earthen vessels, that the excellency of the power may be of God, and not us." We can do nothing of ourselves. It is by anointing that God equips us with spiritual victory. God knows our every word and thought; nothing is hidden from God. With God, all things are possible.

Man, with his limited abilities, can speak and decree many things, yet he cannot withhold a thought from God (Job 42:2). Our minds must be renewed by the word of God. He has proclaimed that He will speak, and His disciples will hear Him. Are you listening? God is speaking to believers today. God wants you to think on things that honor and edify His house. He wants us to meditate on the truth, thinking on His holiness so we will know who He is. With our limited thoughts and with every breath, we need to praise God so that we can have that intimacy with Him.

Prayer: Thank You, Father, for a transformed mind- a mind to worship You and give honor to Your name and live by Your Kingdom principles. Amen.

Step Five: Prove What The Good And Acceptable, And Perfect Will Of God Is

God wants to do a complete work in us. We are His masterpiece, and He has a plan for our lives. We as believers need to know what being complete and perfect is. What has God put in you? What are the desires or unfulfilled thirsts you have to complete for God? Are you listening to what God is calling you to do? God wants us to do His will from the depths of our hearts. He loves us, and He wants us to put no other gods before Him. He demands our love. The word of God reveals His perfect will for us. It is up to us to ask God and search out our life's purpose by prayer and supplication to God.

We must search for that spiritual knowledge that will enable us to tap into that perfect will of God for our lives. Sometimes believers want to compromise with God's plan for their lives. Rather than trying to compromise, start to search out your true purpose by communing with the Holy Spirit, and He will guide you into all truth.

Ask and seek persistently until you get an answer from God. We must be able to hear God's voice in order to know what He is saying by His word. Jesus sought God through prayer and asking if the cup he must drink from would pass him by, but he said, "Not my will but God's will be done." In such a time as this, God wants you in His will by prayer and listening to His voice through His word. We must be able to discern that very still voice or hear a whispering word from the heart of God.

We are to submit to God and resign ourselves to what God wants to do in our lives. Look at what 1 Samuel 3:18 says – "And Samuel told Him every whit, and hid nothing from Him. And he said, It is the Lord: let Him do what seemeth Him good." We can trust God to reveal to us His desires for us. He will reveal to us His will in His own time by His word and our constant prayers. Don't give up hope because God is looking for those who are obedient to His word. Let us seek God, and He will find us for sure.

Prayer: Father, I pray that Your perfect will may be done in my life and on this earth. Help me to be encouraged to stand and do what You called me to do. Amen.

Step Six: Do Not Think Of Yourself More Highly Than You Ought To Think

We as Christians are not to think more of ourselves than what is lawful to think. We grow in grace by faith. Many may grow slower than others, yet the favor of God has no partiality. We are all His workmanship by grace. God has made us soldiers of righteousness by Jesus Christ. We need God's anointing power to be victorious soldiers. The Holy Ghost trains us for battle through the revelation of His word.

He teaches us the power of meditation and humbleness. We can do nothing of ourselves or from our own strength. The scripture reveals in 2 Timothy 2:4 (AMP) "No soldier in active service gets entangled in the [ordinary business] affairs of civilian life; [he avoids them] so that he may please the one who enlisted him to serve."

Our very existence should be to follow after God, meditate on His word, and be obedient to that word as good soldiers, ready to do battle for the cause of righteousness. There are no high-minded officers, just men and women willing by faith to serve God's purpose for us on this earth while we have our strength. We operate in love by grace through Jesus Christ. Should we offend God by lifting ourselves up in pride, believing we have done so much without Christ? Let us not be fools, but sober-minded and full of God's Holy Spirit, endowed with power to get results. Galatians 6:14 says, "But God forbid that I should glory, save in the resurrection of our Lord Jesus Christ, by whom the world is given the right to be saved."

We move and operate in the world, but we are partakers of God's Kingdom. The world has no claim on us. We can live, buy, and sell in the world, yet we are not depending on the world system to make us blessed and secure. Only God can give you blessings and security that is divine, involving no confusion or strings attached. We are led by God's revelation, not by vain and empty talk.

Prayer: *Father, thank You for a renewed mind to think soberly without vain, useless thoughts. We grow in grace by Your righteous direction and guidance of Your Kingdom thinking. Amen.*

Step Seven: Think Soberly According To Your Measure Of Faith

Sober thinking comes when we are aware that God has called us to become united with others by Christ Jesus. The word of God calls us members of the same body, having different functions and gifts serving a vital purpose to keep the body of Christ functioning properly and prospering. As believers, we are expected to operate in faith by love. Faith will not operate if it is not connected to love. Having faith causes us to think, but if that thinking is not coupled by God's love, we are operating outside of God's divine plan.

God put in us a measure of faith, and with that faith, we can discern what the will of God through His word is. The word confirms God's destiny plan for us. If you don't meditate on that word day and night, you won't receive revelation knowledge. Revelation comes from having the joy and love of God in your heart. You cannot have a sick heart and expect to receive God's revelation. Without revelation, our thinking does not line up with God's way of thinking and doing things. Let us examine ourselves to see if we have the mind of Christ.

The Anointed One anoints us, giving us gifts suitable to His pleasure so no man can say that he has a greater portion than another. As Romans 12:10-11 details, let us abide in all earnestness to love one another with "brotherly affection [as members of one family], give preference to one another in honor; never lagging behind in diligence; aglow in the Spirit, enthusiastically serving the Lord;". We must pray for one another and be loving and kind at all times. Don't let anyone cancel out your relationship with God by allowing bitterness or clamor to seep into your heart. Keep a watchful eye. Do good, depart from injustice, seek peace, and pursue it with all men by faith.

__Prayer:__ Lord, I will walk, love, and operate by faith. You have strengthened me by renewing my thinking and by giving me the mind of Christ. In faith, I am connected to the body of Christ by love. Amen.

CHAPTER 47: THE LAWS OF POVERTY

Many people struggle with not having enough, but what do they do with what God has already given them?

We as Christians must know that God believes in work, and even when we ask God for a blessing, He requires something of us. Deuteronomy 11:14 states, "That I will give you the rain of your land in his due season, the first rain and the latter rain, that thou mayest gather in thy corn, and thy wine, and thine oil." The man had to gather what was yielded. He had to work to bring in the blessings. We get confused with working for the blessings, compared to toiling for things of the world.

God has given us the laws that govern this world system. Furthermore, He has shown us a better way if we live by His divine system of laws. God's way are high and lifted up, and His blessings add no sorrows. God doesn't give you a house and then raise the note after you get in it. He doesn't tax you because another company buys your loan. God doesn't bless you and then turn and sell you off to someone else. He is faithful and full of compassion.

Don't meditate on lack because it might happen. Don't allow your neglect of sowing, praying, and giving sneak up on you. Keep praying, don't stop believing the word, and don't stop sowing. Isaac sowed in famine and reaped a harvest that same year.

Let us be like Isaac. Refuse to walk in lack and poverty and hold God to His word. Don't be as the man in Proverbs 24:30 (AMP), as it says, "I went by the field of the lazy man, and by the vineyard of the man void of understanding: "And behold it was grown over with thorns, and nettles were covering its face, and its stone wall was broken down." We as Christians must consider our actions. What are we doing with God's blessings, which He has made us stewards over? You're trying to get more stuff when God has already blessed you mightily beyond what you can ask or think. Let us observe the ants; be diligent to procure your provisions and gather in the harvest. Be encouraged, not lazy and sleeping with regret about what God has made you a steward over.

***Prayer:** Lord, I know You want me to be blessed abundantly. Help me to be a good steward over the blessings You provided. Amen.*

CHAPTER 48: GOD'S FOUR LAWS OF PROSPERITY
"THINK ABUNDANCE"

The First Law: The Law Of Reward

The Bible is very clear. 2 Thessalonians 3:10 (AMP) states, "For even while we were with you, we used to give you this order: if anyone is not willing to work, then he is not to eat, either." When we work, we receive a reward from our labor, whether secular or ministerial. God makes a way for receiving to take place. In any labor, we are responsible for how we govern our blessings in order to get an increase from them. This increase can come from talents, education, investments, and so on. We see an example of this law in Psalm 28:19 (AMP), as it states, "He who cultivates his land will have plenty of bread, but he who follows worthless people and pursuits will have poverty enough."

When we are faithful with what God has given us and not self-centered, God will multiply our efforts and seed sown. He gets pleasure out of the prosperity of His people. Many Christians get tangled up in the idea of quick fixes and quick "get rich" schemes of this world's system without God's divine guidance. As a result, they lose many of their possessions and the hope of having God's best without sorrow accompanying it.

You must wait on the Holy Ghost and allow Him to direct all your dealings in this earthly realm. He will teach and guide you in every area of your life. God promised to direct you by His Holy Spirit. He will tell us where to go, who to visit, whose house to bless, the ministry to give to, and who to trust. He assures us to abide with those who are just and faithful. We will help them to be blessed, bringing more blessings on us, as detailed in Luke 10:7. God wants to reward us. He doesn't want to take anything from us. It is all based on the law of reward. When we reward people for good, we receive good unto our family and possessions.

Some Christians refuse to work for the benefit of the Kingdom. They'd rather become gossipers and busybodies, walking in a disorderly manner and doing evil in the sight of God. God has no pleasure in fools. We must eat our bread in quietness and be not weary in well-doing (2 Thessalonians 3:11-13 AMP).

Prayer: Thank You, Father, for a reward of mercy. Help me to know how to work with my hands, laboring to build Your kingdom and use the gifts You have given me. Amen.

The Second Law: The Law Of Release

We must release for the increase. Scripture says that he to whom more has been given, Christ expects more from. The word also says that the liberal soul shall be made fat. We as children of God are expected to be lenders and not borrowers. We are the distributors of goods to the poor and the needy. We are walking and living an abundant life through Christ Jesus. Let us be the just and faithful stewards of God's inheritance because we live in the blessings of Abraham.

Let's read Proverbs 11:24-25 (AMP). It states, "There are those who [generously] scatter abroad, and those who withhold more than is fitting or what is justly due, but it results only in want. The liberal person shall be enriched, and he who waters shall himself be watered." The Holy Spirit lets us know that in order to increase, we must give out of a willing heart. When we withhold what is just from God and man, we violate God's law of increase.

When our giving or not giving becomes a hindrance to the work of God and ministry, God lets us know by allowing us to experience lack in our lives, relationships, and finances. We cannot hold our hands so tightly that nothing can come in or go out.

When we do that which is good and right in God's eyes, we receive favor. We will not fall. The righteous shall be recompensed on Earth, but the sinner loses all hope of receiving from God. And if the righteous are barely saved, what will become of the ungodly and wicked?

The Lord uses godly men and women to teach us. If we refuse to adhere to that wisdom, it is our fault alone. Let us walk as wise children of God and not followers of foolish babblings. God's word has a purpose. We are not just hearing the word for the sake of only hearing it. We must ask God. You must ask God what your purpose for being here is so you can be liberal and increase in His favor to live an abundant life.

Prayer: Thank You, Father, for enabling me to be a generous soul. Make me a distributor so that I may be blessed to give more and more. Amen.

The Third Law: The Law Of Receiving

The Bible teaches us the laws of receiving as the foundation for all God has proclaimed. We must expect God by faith to hear us, to protect us, and to take care of us. Without expectation, we have no hope. Without hope, we have no faith. Without faith, we have no confidence, which has great recompense of reward. We must live in expectations of God promises and provisions for us hear in this time and age.

Now is the designated time to look for redemption and great reward. We have to receive the promises. If not, what do we need patience for? God's will is that we hear and obey the word by faith. The will of God is His word. To receive the promises is to receive the word, and God's word will perform that which it is sent to accomplish. When we receive that word, we are able to walk in the authority that that word brings.

God said, "All things are made alive by the word of His power. His power is in the word. In order to receive the blessings, we must follow the law of receiving. Luke 6:38 states, "Give, and it shall be given unto you; good measure, pressed down, and shaken together, and running over, shall men give into your bosom. For with the same measure that ye mete withal it shall be measured to you again."

To get out of any situation, God is saying give and sow for it is the law of the breakthrough for us all. The law of receiving works at all times, but not without expectation. Peter and John were walking toward the temple, and a crippled man saw them and asked for alms. Peter looked at him and said, "Look on us." The crippled man looked at them, expecting something. He looked in expectation, not knowing what he would receive. He didn't receive silver and gold, but he received the power to walk. In other words, he had the power to change his position and take authority of his situation. His faith changed his life forever. He believed his way out of lack into complete wholeness.

***Prayer:** Thank You, Father, for enabling me to receive from my expectations of faith in Your promises. I want to be a giver, expecting the power of Your word to sustain me in every area of my life. Amen.*

The Fourth Law: The Law Of Reciprocation

God wants to use His people to establish His Kingdom on the earth. Yes, He blesses us with all sufficiency, but what is the purpose of it all? The only reason God would put abundance into our hands is to establish His covenant on the earth.

It costs to preach the word. It costs to translate scriptures and to travel all over the globe. God knows what you need, and He gives you the provisions to carry out His mission on Earth. We as Christians are the channel by which God gets those provisions to His people. We should never see ourselves as giving just to a man or woman preaching the word, but we should revere our giving as unto the Lord. He will reward and pay what is right in due time if we faint not.

When God blesses you, you should have the desire to bless Him back. God doesn't want us to seek after Him just for the benefits and increase. God has already told us to seek Him and His Kingdom first and His righteousness; He will add all the things to us.

Look at Mark 4:20, as it states, "And these are they which are sown on good ground; such as hear the word, and receive it, and bring forth fruit, some thirtyfold, some sixty, and some an hundred."

When God blesses us, He expects us to bear good fruit. We are known by our fruits. How do you respond after God has done great things in your life? Do you do great things for others? God always keep His word. He does not lie or repent. We must realize that we did not make ourselves, nor can we sustain our own lives. You need God, no matter how much you think you've got it or how much you think you can do it on your own. Don't be a fool. God made us, not we ourselves. John 15:16 states, "Ye have not chosen me, but I have chosen you, and ordained you, that ye should go and bring forth fruit, and that your fruit should remain: that whatsoever ye shall ask of the Father in my name, He may give it you."

Prayer: *I thank You, Father, for putting in me a giving spirit so that I may bear fruit that remains good fruit of covenant blessings. Amen.*

CHAPTER 49: THE HOLY SPIRIT WITNESSES TO US AS TEACHER, LEADER, SPIRIT OF TRUTH, AND COMFORTER

God's Holy Spirit lives within us believers because we confess Jesus as our Lord and Savior by faith. The world cannot receive the Holy Spirit because there is no enlightenment given to them about Him. The world doesn't know Him because their hearts, which are their inner beings, are far from Him. He is not in them, living and speaking, because of unbelief.

The Holy Spirit bears witness with our spirits that we are the children of God (Romans 8:16). God places his spirit inside the believer. You are connected to the power source by spiritual adoption through Jesus Christ, God's son. We became joint heirs and are ushered into the everlasting sonship of God through the power of God's resurrected son. How loved and blessed we are to have God's inheritance available to us. God cares so much for us that He gave His only begotten son to die for us. Now Jesus is a part of us totally by grace. Look at Galatians 4:6, as it states, "And because ye are sons, God hath sent forth the spirit of His son into your hearts, crying Abba, Father." God is our Father, and we are adopted sons because we have God's spirit in our hearts by Christ Jesus. You received this adoption when you called on Jesus as the Lord of your salvation and Savior of your life.

Surely, He is our Father – purely spiritual first, and in all other areas included by faith. The faith that comes alive by obedience to God's word (laws and precepts). We have received a gift that no other creature can receive. God has adopted us into His family so that we may receive the promises of all that He has to offer "according to His riches in glory by Christ Jesus". These wonderful promises are sealed by the blood of God's only son Jesus. God truly has given us His commandments so that we may become rooted in this sonship by obedience of the word, so we will not fail like Adam and Eve.

God has placed this seal of salvation by the Holy Spirit so that we are forever sons and daughters of all promises, all heavenly dwellings, and blessings for He is able to perform His word by the power of His might. No demon in hell or on Earth can prevent the love of God from taking effect, being demonstrated, and manifested in the lives of His children. He has given His Spirit to us, dwelling on the inside of us and working in us, through us, and with us by the word of His power. We can relate to the word of Isaiah 63:16, as it states, "Doubtless thou art our Father, though Abraham be ignorant of us, and Israel acknowledge us not; Thou, O Lord, art our Father, our Redeemer: Thy name is from everlasting." We have that same connection to God as gentiles, and we should not be called outcasts. God sent his son for all mankind so that we may have the advantages and benefits of any blood sons because the blood flowed from outside of us to within us by the piercing of the Savior's side on the cross.

We have received him by the blood covenant that was made to all mankind from the foundation of the world. Romans 8:17 states, "And if children, then heirs; heirs of God, and joint-heirs with Christ; if so be that we suffer with Him, that we may be also glorified together."

Prayer: *Thank You, Father, for the witness of the Holy Spirit that we are sons and joint heirs of Your promises and that Your Spirit dwells in our hearts as we cry, "Abba Father." Amen.*

Holy Spirit As Teacher

We as children of God must recognize that we have God's spirit to assist us in every area of need and substance. The problem today begins in the minds and hearts of God's people. We have been led to believe that all we have to do is think positively and everything will work itself out. We have denied the existence of a significant other: the God Head, the Holy Ghost.

God confirms His word by letting us know who this powerful individual is. He has been around since the foundation of the world when God spoke and said, "Let us make man." We know because He dwells in us through Christ Jesus. He speaks spiritual things to the believer. He helps you understand the anointing of God's wisdom and power by instructing the believer on the unseen things of the Most High.

Let us look at 1 Corinthians 2:13, as it says, "Which things also we speak, not in the words which man's wisdom teacheth, but which the Holy Ghost teacheth; comparing spiritual things with spiritual." You may ask what this means to the believer.

The spirit of the world cannot teach men spiritual things. We can only receive those spiritual instructions from God's spirit. You can receive spiritual knowledge, spiritual discernment, spiritual wisdom, and spiritual benefits, which are freely given to us by God. This is how we know what is rightfully ours in Christ Jesus. The Holy Spirit reveals it to us and teaches us how to benefit from it by faith.

The advantages we have, which are given when we are in a favorable position with God, enable us to receive instructions in wisdom from the Spirit teacher. He reveals to believers God's divine anointing that enables us to receive all truths and believe all things by abiding in His promises. We must recognize His divine anointing. 1 John 2:27 (AMP) states, "As for you, the anointing [the special gift, the preparation] which you received from Him remains [permanently] in you, and you have no need for anyone to teach you. But just as His anointing teaches you [giving you insight through the presence of the Holy Spirit] about all things, and is true and is not a lie, and just as His anointing has taught you, you must remain in Him [being rooted in Him, knit to Him]."

Prayer: Father, thank You for being a Teacher of truth, who reveals to me the seen and unseen blessings of Your glory through Christ Jesus. Amen.

Spirit as Leader and Guide

The Holy Spirit shows His power by taking leadership in carrying out the will of God's justice for His chosen people. We as believers are God's chosen people. The Holy Ghost reveals to us all truth, all that He hears from the Father, and all things to come. He gets His mandates from our Heavenly Father. He does not speak of Himself. He makes no demands for Himself, and He executes every direction of authority to the letter, as given by God Himself. He is the executer of righteousness and divine justice, according to John 16:13.

The Holy Ghost knows where we are and what we are doing at all times. In fact, He directs our movements, as God determines our positions in life. As we earnestly seek God and meditate on His plans for our lives and seek His face by praying constantly, He helps us to understand our purpose and His vision for our lives, as the Holy Ghost assures us that we are operating within God's plans. God directs and positions us before men and women that have like-mindedness and a desire to carry out God's purpose and establish His covenant on the earth. God's divine plans shall be done on the earth by Kingdom principles and His divine leadership, according to Acts 10:19. God determines your position and authority and makes provisions for it. He makes the promises for the vision, and He gives gifts unto men without repentance.

You cannot have a vision unless God puts it inside of your spirit. When God decides that the vision must come forth, He makes sure that all doubt, legality, discrimination, or hesitation is done away with. We must resolve to allow the Holy Spirit to set God's plans in order for leadership to take place by divine order in all that we establish in Christ Jesus. If we do not allow God to build the house (the foundation of His vision), we who build it labor in vain. God knows what work he calls us to. Acts 13:2 (AMP) states, "While they were serving the Lord and fasting, the Holy Spirit said, 'Set apart for Me Barnabas and Saul (Paul) for the work to which I have called them."

Prayer: *Father, thank You for the leadership of the Holy Ghost. He guides us to our destiny by Your directions and gives us the authority to operate by Your divine orders. Amen.*

Holy Spirit As The Life Giver

The term "quickens" is defined by Strong's Concordance in the Greek as that which "vitalizes", "makes alive", and "gives life". God proclaims to us in His word that we have the spirit of Christ living on the inside of us. John 6:63 (AMP) states, "It is the spirit who gives life; the flesh conveys no benefit [it is of no account]. The words I have spoken to you are spirit and life [providing eternal life]."

We must be able to receive this truth. Only those who are ready to go to the next level in the Lord, and those who have renewed their mind by meditating on the word, will receive the truth. The truth is that many of Christ's disciples left to follow Him because of the word of His power. To be like God means to think like God. The spirit provides the super to our natural as He dwells on the inside of the believer. The flesh wars against God's spirit, but you must not give in to the tangible, as the word says, "Blessed are those who have not seen yet believe". You cannot trust in the flesh to give you the answers that are spiritually discerned. Only God can transform your thoughts and change your destiny as He directs and we follow after His guidance. We must understand God's divine plan and revelation according to His great pleasures.

Without God's Spirit one is already dead to the ways of God and there is no relationship or fellowship with the Father. The world's system does not have the answers to spiritual matters because there is no knowledge of God's love and mercy. Carnal ways and beliefs cannot provide solutions that comfort, heal sickness, cast out demons, heal diseases, mend broken hearts, or restore relationships. God's Kingdom system gives life and restores us into the fullness of Christ Jesus. The ways and means of this world system can only bring temporary benefits for a few days, but God can heal us for a lifetime in wholeness and peace, not as the world gives, but only as God's eternal love can give.

The Bible reveals to us in Romans 8:11, "But if the Spirit of him that raised up Jesus from the dead dwell in you, he that raised up Christ from the dead shall also quicken your mortal bodies by his spirit that dwelleth in you." This day are we risen in Christ by his precious blood of salvation that quicken our lives from dead works unto good works. We are not born of corruptible seed but incorruptible seed. Let us be ready by living a life of faith, following as true disciples, and expecting wonderful things that will increase our faith and magnify God in our lives. We will desire what God wants and follow His lead every step of the way by being obedient in all He requires of us.

We are members of the new order of God by Christ Jesus, who has made us heirs of the promise through the Father's will forever. 2 Corinthians 3:6 states, "Who also hath made us able ministers of the new testament; not of the letter, but of the spirit: for the letter killeth, but the spirit giveth life."

Prayer: *Thank You, Father, for Your Holy Spirit, the Life Giver. He enables us to live a sin-free life by quickening our mortal bodies from dead works to living a life depending on Your eternal promises. Amen.*

Holy Spirit As The Spirit of Truth

In today's society, many people don't know what truth is. Daily, we are bombarded with untruths about people's lives, entertainment, ratings, certain portrayals of stereotypes in movies, and the news media. No wonder the family is falling apart. There is no stability in morality in the world system, and they are trying to live what this system proclaims as normal and true. How do we avoid such traps of the evil one? We are in the world, but not of the world. Let us live as the giver of life has intended with His master plan for our lives.

John 14:17 says, "Even the spirit of truth; whom the world cannot receive, because it seeth him not, neither knoweth him: but ye know him; for he dwelleth with you, and shall be in you". If we follow after God's teachings (the Holy Bible), God tells us that the spirit of truth dwells in us (he is not in the world; the world can't see or know him). We are the instruments and vessels that God uses to demonstrate His power on Earth. We are the vessels that speak His will for His people. We the church of believers proclaiming the word of God's power have a job to do. If you will let your light shine through the darkness of this world, so many souls will be saved and able to survive what is coming on this earth. We know the spirit of Truth will show us things to come. Nothing will be able to sneak up on the children who are in obedience to God. We are chosen to warn others of this area of deceit so that we may save God's harvest of souls because the fields are white and ready to be harvested. "Pray that God will send laborers into the fields to gather them before it's too late." Many may hear, and many may not. 1 John 4:6 (AMP) states, "We [who teach God's word] are from God [energized by the Holy Spirit], and whoever knows God [through personal experience] listens to us [and has a deeper understanding of Him]. Whoever is not of God does not listen to us. By this we know [without any doubt] the spirit of truth [motivated by God] and the spirit of error [motivated by Satan]."

Prayer: Thank You, God, for the spirit of Truth, who guides me and shows me things to come so that my light of understanding may be clear. Amen.

Holy Spirit As Our Comforter

The Holy Spirit comforts all believers. We are not without peace of mind and love. We are not held responsible for our wrongdoings because God gave us love by the comfort of the Holy Spirit as He obeys the orders of the Father. He always does what God says, and He reveals to us the meaning of what He says. We know that our spirits have contact with the Holy Spirit. Together, they enable us to discern and hear from God in every area of our lives. Jesus has already prayed to the Father so that we could receive the Comforter. Jesus gave word that another Comforter would come after he left to return to the mercy seat. Let us read John 14:16, as it states, "And I will pray the Father, and He shall give you another Comforter, that he may abide with you for ever…"

The Comforter will abide with you forever. The Comforter will abide with us and in us forever for greater is He that is in us than he that is in the world.

The Comforter will bring to our remembrance the word when we need it. He teaches us what to say for peace, love, grace, forgiveness, and all things needed for the children of God. How beautiful that is. God loves us so much until He provided a way for us to be comfortable on the earth, not the physical comforts only but provisions unseen, such as love, peace, grace, and finances.

I am excited about the testimony of Holy Ghost. He testifies about the goodness of Christ.

Let's read John 15:26 (AMP), as it states, "But when the Helper (Comforter, Advocate, Intercessor—Counselor, Strengthener, Standby) comes, whom I will send to you from the Father, that is the spirit of Truth who comes from the Father, He will testify and bear witness about Me."

He is an advocate, a great helper whenever we need Him. He stands as intercessor for our weaknesses and shortcomings. He loves us unconditionally. The Comforter strengthens us for every situation we have to face. He wants us to win every time. That is why we are more than conquerors by Christ Jesus.

The Holy Spirit will also convict the world of sin. John 16:8-11 states, "And when he is come, he will reprove the world of sin, and of righteousness, and of judgment: Of sin, because they believe not on me; Of righteousness, because I go to my Father, and ye see me no more; Of judgment, because the prince of this world is judged."

Meditation on the Word BRINGS THE MIND OF CHRIST

Prayer: *Father, thank You for the Comforter, who keeps us in perfect peace. He is advocate, strengthener, and helper forever. Amen.*

The Purpose For The Anointing

God anoints His people to do a work for Him. He anointed Saul to be a king of Israel. He told Samuel to anoint Gideon to be a captain over his inheritance, according to 1 Samuel 10:1. God gives His anointed powers to those who have a vision for God's work and business. Many people work, but is it God's business they are doing? All work should be God's business for the believer because you are on an assignment for God.

Toiling is not God's intended plan for us. Your day-to-day job is an assignment for you given by God. God has put you there for a specific purpose; therefore, you have to do God's will as long as you are there. You will set the atmosphere and climate for the right leadership to thrive. You are the one that will pull the staff together in times of confusion. You will be the encourager for everyone you come in contact with. That same position or job may fold, and the company may go under. This is time you must say to God, "God, I don't have this job you gave me anymore, so what's the next assignment you have for me?" We as believers depend too much on man's abilities and resources instead of depending on God's promises, Kingdom living, and Kingdom business. We can't depend on this world's resources; we must depend on God's provisions. We must trust God with our money and allow Him to multiply it based on Kingdom principles. For too long, we have we endured hardship and lack because of how the world's system has dealt with us and our finances. The job you have cannot afford you a comfortable living. The system is always taking as much as possible and giving you little by little and what it thinks you need. Let us as believers trust God at His word and become lenders, not borrowers, according to God's plan. God has confirmed in His word that we are to administer seed to the sower and multiply the seed sown.

Anointing has many functions to do God's will. We see that anointing operates when you become sick. We can anoint the sick with oil by prayer, rubbing in the oil, and the sick will recover immediately by faith. The anointing teaches us all things. We receive enlightenment and witty ideas. We become highly creative and full of wisdom because the anointing abides in us. The anointing teaches us truth and never lies. His teaching causes us to have confidence and not be ashamed, according to John 2:27-28.

Prayer: Father, thank You for giving us Your anointing to work in every area of our lives: to heal, to know wisdom, and to walk in the truth of Your word so that we may abide in Your confidence and not be ashamed forever. Amen.

Divine Ability Through The Anointing

God has sworn in His own anger and declared an indignation against the enemies of his people, all believers. The world's system today is determined to cast down God's anointed, but we are held up in fruitfulness through God's enlightenment about our oppressors. Surely, God will avenge His own. We shall become a people set apart and strengthened to ensure that the enemies of God and all unbelievers will be cut off and destroyed by way of the anointing.

We must repent and prepare ourselves to decree recompense for all we have lost and all the devil has stolen from us. God will restore the years the canker worm has destroyed. Isaiah 10:27 (AMP) states, "So it will be in that day, that the burden of the Assyrian will be removed from your shoulders and his yoke from your neck. The yoke will be broken because of the fat."

God is saying that His people will no longer be oppressed by their enemies. We as believers shall have restoration of the blessings by the hand of God. He shall give us recompense for all we have lost. He will give us riches, lands, blessings, favor, plenteousness, and health. We are fat with His revelation and the blessings so that no one will be able to put any oppression or undue toil on us again by way of anointing. Anointing destroys any yoke, confusion, lack, poverty, ignorance, oppression, and even financial hardships. When you receive the revelation of how God has blessed you, you won't be the same. Your mind becomes renewed, and your life takes on new meaning and purpose. You are valuable to God.

You don't have to suffer for anything. Anointing destroys the yoke of anything that makes you uncomfortable. You are no longer discouraged; you are encouraged by faith in Jesus Christ. You now have the divine ability to operate in the power of God's might.

Prayer: *Father, I thank You for the anointing power in my life. You have taken poverty, lack, ignorance, and financial hardship out of my life forever. Amen.*

The Force of the Anointing

When we speak, teach, or preach the word of God, let us do it by the ability God gives us. We cannot take credit for God's ability; He gives us the power to stand in all circumstances. We cannot carry out God's plan by our own force; we can only carry out His plan and precepts by the Holy Spirit teaching us what the Father would have us do. When we allow the Holy Spirit to lead us in our teaching and preaching, the power of God comes in and saves the sinner and convicts the believer for His sake. When we don't let the Holy Ghost do it, we hinder God's hand to build up and restore broken lives and mend broken hearts.

The love of God can only flow through us when the Holy Ghost gives us spiritual refinishing. Let us glorify God and take no honor for ourselves. The force of the anointing must come from God's enabling power, His super on our natural. God uses us as channels to work miracles in the lives of believers and those who need to receive salvation.

God's power is called "dunamus" in Greek, meaning "mighty deed" or "worker of miracles, power, and strength". We can operate in this same "dunamus" by God's anointing on our lives. If we allow the anointing to take place before we try to handle the works of the Holy Spirit, we will win every time. Let us look at Matthew 25:15 (AMP), as it states, "To one he gave five talents, to another, two, and to another, one, each according to his own ability; and then he went on his journey." Can God trust you to use your strength, ability, and abundance to carry out His plan and purpose for your life? He gave these three believers talents or money to increase the Kingdom. As a steward, what are you doing with God's money? Are you working only to take care of your needs? God wants us to use the blessings He gives us to establish His Kingdom on the earth. Can He trust you to use His money for His purpose and benefit? We have never lacked anything following God's plans for our lives.

***Prayer:** Thank You, Father, for giving me the ability, force, and power to do Your will and follow Your examples for my life and not operate by my own strength. Amen.*

Power Demonstrated By Love

God expects us as believers to know that His power is not just for us to hope and shout about without living the life. Believers must live life in demonstration of God's abilities and power operating from within them.

You can speak the word and proclaim the word, but until you see the actual results of the word spoken by faith, the power has not been activated. 1 Corinthians 4:20 (AMP) states, "For the Kingdom of God consists of and is based on not talk but on power." We must awaken our potential within us in order to tap into the divine, supernatural ability God wants us to operate in. We as children of God must be proactive in our living and giving, even in the battling of the forces of wickedness in this world. Our way of doing things must line up with Kingdom principles and God's way of doing things. How can one preach against adultery and at the same time be an adulterer? God does not find pleasure in fools. Jesus set the example for us to follow by saying that we are in the world but not of the world. We have the mind of Christ, a mind of excellence, doing what God wants us to do willingly and with a spirit of perfection.

We want God to love us and give us the desires of our heart yet we want to live within the world system, doubting that God can work out our problems and situations.

Do you trust God to be all you want Him to be for you and your love ones? Walk in love so that the power of God through faith can work on your behalf. God is love. He doesn't just exhibit love; He is love. Let us do the word and not just hear it. Bring the word to life in your daily life and in all that you do. We must put it to practice and exercise our abilities in the power of excellence as we operate in the mind of Christ. We must exhibit the character of kindness, mercy, gentleness, faithfulness, and charity. If we are to represent God, let us represent Him in word, deed, and power through His son Jesus Christ. Let His presence grace us with His glory forever.

Prayer: Father, thank You for enabling me to show You power in my living and not just by words f or in You is an excellent spirit. Amen.

Power To Become The Sons Of God

When we receive Christ as our personal Savior, we become the "Sons of God", male or female. God gave us the power to act and be like Him. We are co-creators on the earth, full of the power of God. Jesus, the son of God, is our brother. He has set us free, and whom the Son sets free is free indeed.

Now we have the privilege and rights to command, work, and set free the broken-hearted and the oppressed by the power of God. All we have to do is trust God and rely on Him to carry out every promise by covenant He has ever given us by His divine word. We will reap the benefits thereof. John 1:12 states, "But as many as received him, to them gave he power to become the sons of God, even to them that believe on his name…"

All we have to do is believe. You must believe that God has given and confirmed your destiny plan by His salvation plan.

We know that Jesus did not come on his own. It was God the Father who sent him, and he did nothing without the Father telling and guiding him on what to do. The name of Jesus has the power to save your soul and cleanse you from all unrighteousness. God gave us the power to become His sons by faith in the name of Jesus.

The Bible states that we do not owe our birth, our blood, or the will of the flesh to any man, but to God for we are born of God in every word and divine order (John 1:13 AMP). It is by the grace of God that He has given us such a glorious opportunity to become the Sons of God. And we know that Christ Jesus dwelt among us as a man and suffered every temptation as man, yet he did not sin. Let us abide in him and his word for God has given us this power to become true Sons of God. What a wonderful gift to be loved.

Prayer: Lord, I will trust You, love You, and depend on You forever more as a son trusts a natural father. Thank You for the power to reign in Your authority. Amen.

God's Spiritual Blessings

God's love for us causes blessings to flow in our lives. We as believers should know that God loves us unconditionally. We sometimes allow the devil to creep in and deceive us into doubting God's love. God will turn the curses that Satan tries to put on you into blessings when you exhibit your faith. God is not one to forget our labors of love. He will give us peace and the assurance that we will not be harmed by our enemies. When God defeats our enemies, they cannot return to haunt or oppress us. He restores us completely: mind, body, and spirit.

The Lord wants us to have clean hands and a clear heart. He wants to dwell on the inside of us for we are His temple, a habitation for praise. God has confirmed His salvation in us by the Holy Spirit for a blessing to all believers.

We shall receive God's blessings from Christ Jesus and righteousness from the God of our salvation, according to Psalm 24:5. The Lord will fight our battles; He will provide recompense for us from our oppressors. Let us glorify the King of Kings and the Lord of Lords. He will fight for us and win the battle, and His glory will come forth to his people. We would have fallen and been consumed had God not defended us in battles. He has given us a way to escape the snares of the enemy.

We can call on the name of the Lord, and He will hear us. He is all-powerful, our Deliverer. Of whom shall we be afraid? Psalm 124:8 states, "Our help is in the name of the Lord, who made Heaven and Earth." Blessings flow from God. He has given us life, more abundant life than we could ever imagine.

He has given us Agape life, "Zoë" life, a life of joy, peace, and victories over every problem or situation we will ever face. We have God's assurance of protection forever. God has made a covenant with us as sons and daughters. Everything He has is made available to us by Christ Jesus. He has given us spiritual riches and physical riches. Proverbs 10:22 states, "The blessing of the Lord, it maketh rich, and He addeth no sorrow with it." We don't have to labor for it. He gives it freely.

Prayer: Father, thank You for all spiritual blessings. Your covenant promises are always ready to help, protect, and give life to those who believe and are obedient to Your word. Amen.

God's Divine Favor

The Lord will exalt the believer; He will set us up for glory and honor and put us on display. The wicked will see the marvelous wonders and power of God's divine favor on us in every area of our lives. The Holy Spirit will defend our cause and execute vengeance on all our oppressors and anyone that has done us any injustice. God is a God of justice, and we will wait on Him for our deliverance. He will have mercy upon those who love His statutes and commandments. He will hear every cry and prayer that we utter. He will surely hear and respond.

The scriptures reveal to us that "the Lord will restore the years the canker worm has taken away". He will give us favor and shower us with the wealth of the wicked; the blessings are laid up for us. The wicked are literally working for those who love the Lord. He will put kings at our feet, and we will build the waste places. God has declared it by the word of His power. Read Isaiah 60:11, as it states, "Therefore thy gates shall be open continually; they shall not be shut day nor night; that men may bring unto thee the forces of the Gentiles, and that their kings may be brought." God has given us dominion over kings and nations and all that He wants to establish here on Earth in our time.

Let us get ready to do great exploits for God. He has shown us favor and healed our hearts and the waste places. We are sons and daughters that bring delight to a Father. Lift up a shout and know that the Lord is good.

God wants to plant us in place, so we can carry out His assignment for our lives. He has a plan for you, and no devil in hell will be able to stop the destiny plan God has for your life. God proclaims His word in Jeremiah 32:41, as it states, "Yea, I will rejoice over them to do them good, and I will plant them in this land assuredly with my whole heart and with my whole soul."

God has promised His people good. He will not stop until every promise is fulfilled. Let us trust God to know what is right and just for us. He has the plan and has given us purpose. Rather than trying to put together what you think God wants for your life, you must seek out the purpose rather than trying to put together your own agenda. We owe it all to God's mercy and grace. We must trust and seek Him for guidance as He leads us from faith to faith and glory to glory.

Prayer: Father, thank You for divine favor on my life. You cared enough about me to bless me, protect me, and give me Your word that justice will follow me. You will direct my paths in life for Your covenant's sake. Amen.

With Favor, God Hears Us

We are not to fight our own battles. The battle is not ours. We as believers must trust God to bring justice in time of need. If we wait on Him, He will come through for us. We are not to get discouraged and fainthearted when things don't seem to be working in our favor. God is waiting for us to turn the situation over to Him. Man's extremities are God's opportunities. Look at Isaiah 30:18, as it states, "And therefore will the Lord wait, that He may be gracious unto you, and therefore will He be exalted, that He may have mercy upon you: for the Lord is a God of judgment: blessed are all they that wait for Him." The Lord is gracious and full of lovingkindness towards His people. He will hear you when you call. He will answer your prayers and give sound wisdom and guidance. He will cause us to receive revelation knowledge and spiritual insight in our businesses and daily activities.

We can rest in God's assurance that He will avenge us against our adversaries. Those who have made us ashamed will be utterly destroyed. There will be no more sorrow nor despair; He will restore us to our rightful state. We shall have no fear; our hands shall give and spare not. Our houses, land, and the seed of our bodies are blessed. God loves us, and He wants the best for us. By the power of His might has he sustained us and brought deliverance to His own. The word says, "The Lord thy God in the midst of thee is mighty; He will save, He will rejoice over thee with joy; He will rest in His love, He will joy over thee with singing" (Zephaniah 3:17). The Lord will gather us and give us rest and peace. God will forgive all our iniquities; He will remember our wrongdoings no more. He will keep us in His righteousness. All who trust in the Lord shall be united in God's family and receive fullness of joy.

Prayer: *Father, thank You for hearing my cry. I am Your chosen remnant; You have filled me with everlasting joy and blotted out my transgressions. Amen.*

Prosperity Revealed To The Believers

God established His covenant with the seed of Abraham. All generations of believers flow from this original covenant. God promised Abraham that his seeds would prosper if they obeyed His word and kept the covenant after their exit out of Egypt. What is this revealed prosperity for us today as believers? Deuteronomy 29:9 states, "Keep therefore the words of this covenant, and do them, that ye may prosper in all that ye do." That word "prosper" in the Hebrew is tselach, meaning "expert", "to be intelligent", "instruct (make to understand; wisdom", "make wise", "behave wisely", or "guide wittingly". The covenant revealed the prosperity according to God's plan of receiving all He has for us by wisdom, inventions, and witty ideas. We are to be experts and excellent in all that we do because the anointing will instruct us to do it God's way. The prosperity was not only for money and possessions, but for solving problems and giving instruction to bring one out of darkness into the understanding of doing great exploits.

We are Kingdom-minded and full of power by God's might. We are vessels for God to pour in revelation knowledge of the seen and the unseen. God wants to get us out of our comfort zone in order to expand our mental capacity.

The more we are exposed to what seems to be impossible and out of our reach, the more we will be able to see what God has for us to do. He shows us part of the vision and takes us through a process of getting the whole picture, but once He has demonstrated to us the miraculous by seeing someone who has walked in it; He can get us to walk in what He has for us on a higher level. God wants us to think big. We must operate from the viewpoint of His super on our natural.

When Moses died, God gave Joshua a charge to continue on the mission with the people. He promised Joshua that He would be with Him. So is it for us today. The decisions and the process of growth to expand God's Kingdom are more vital than ever today. God commanded Joshua to take courage and be cheerful. Don't be dismayed for He is with us right now.

Prayer: Father, thank You for revealed knowledge of our inheritance. Guide us in Thy wisdom, courage, and favor forever. Amen.

Living In The Spirit (Prayer 1)

We as believers are justified by faith. We are Abraham's descendants because we believe God and it brings about our conversion and gaining our salvation through Christ Jesus. The Bible reveals to us that if we believe God's promises, he will surely bring all things to the light. Romans 5:1 states, "Therefore being justified by faith, we have peace with God through our Lord Jesus Christ…"

We have this peace in earthen vessels, and God will provide comfort, blessings, peace, love, and all things for our good. No good thing will be kept from His children.

The spirit of God comes in to cleanse us from all unrighteousness, wash us, and satisfy using the word by Christ Jesus. We must continue in the word, meditating on that word every day and night. Within God's own plan of salvation, we are sanctified and justified by His anointing. Our faith causes God's love to abide in our hearts by Christ Jesus. Let us follow God's plan of salvation by accepting God's divine love for us all. Let's read Ph 3:9, as it states, "And be found in Him, not having mine own righteousness, which is of the law, but that which is through the faith of Christ, the righteousness which is of God by faith…"

So, faith is the key to our obtaining the righteousness of God because after we receive Christ as our personal Savior, we may not feel any differently or think any differently at that moment. It is not about your feelings at all. You must trust God to do what we can't see or feel by faith. We have the righteousness of Jesus because he gave his life so that we may receive his righteousness, something we did not have and does not belong to us, yet we received it from God's son. The evidence is clear that Christ is the key component of divine blessings of God. Let's look at Mark 9:23, as it states, "Jesus said unto him, If thou canst believe, all things are possible to him that believeth." We must believe God for divine health, divine blessings, and all that He has for us.

Prayer: Thank You, Father, for giving me faith by love. I am full of the righteousness and love of Christ Jesus. He loves me because he gave himself for me. Amen.

Living in the Spirit (Prayer 2)

God wants us to be faithful in Christ Jesus. God is our Father, and He has blessed us through Jesus. He has set us in heavenly places and has given us all things and spiritual blessings to enjoy. God the Blesser holds success and dominion in His hands. God has given it all to us, His children. Ephesians 1:4 states, "According as he hath chosen us in Him before the foundation of the world, that we should be holy and without blame before Him in love." God chose us before we even knew Him. He has a destiny plan for us. Our lives are foreordained to do the will of our Father. All He wants is for us to be willing to step into our position, so God can use us. We must rise and position ourselves to do the work of our Father as dear children. God's word is His will. Let us walk in faith by grace and receive the provisions He has provided in abundance for all time.

God has given us wisdom, witty ideas, and courage to stand in His divine counsel of peace and grace. We know that our flesh profits nothing, but the spirit of God living on the inside of us gives us life eternal by God's divine mercy. Look at 1 Peter 3:18, as it states, "For Christ also hath once suffered for sins, the just for the unjust that he might bring us to God, being put to death in the flesh, but quickened by the spirit…"

The spirit of God working on the inside brings life to our dead works and defeats the flesh of our selfish desires. By receiving God's word that gives life to our spirits, we are not led by the flesh that has no profit and is dead in unrighteousness. We cannot trust in the flesh; if we do, we are empowered to fail. Let us follow the spirit of life, the word of God that causes us to be empowered to succeed.

God the Blesser knows what we need, and He provides all that we need. He gives us power to accomplish His will and succeed. He positions our lives and causes us to live by faith so the blessings will flow because our faith operates by love.

Prayer: Thank You, Father, for quickening my spirit and filling me with life. You profit me in power, love, and blessings. Amen.

The First Phase Of God's Revealing Knowledge

God has given you spiritual insight. He wants you to know what your benefits and rewards are in this dispensation of truth. You must ask yourself some questions. How do you stand in relationship with Jesus Christ and why do you go to church? Are you merely following blind tradition or are you serious about expecting God to move and execute manifested evidence of His love and power in your life? I don't know about you, but when God tells me by His stripes I am healed, I expect to receive healing in my body. I want to have a repentant heart and not be filled with empty hardness of heart or a life that has no profit.

God knows our every thought and deed; we cannot hide anything from Him. God has a grace that follows us if we are obedient to His word. Let's read Romans 16:25, as it states, "Now to Him that is of power to stablish you according to my gospel, and the preaching of Jesus Christ, according to the revelation of the mystery, which was kept secret since the world began, But now is made manifest, and by the scriptures of the prophets, according to the commandment of the everlasting God, made known to all nations for the obedience of faith…"

We are to believe in the Lord, and He will establish us. If we believe His chosen men and women that He has assigned to pour into our spirits, so shall we prosper. We cannot work the wonders of God if we do not believe. Our works are of no value if we cannot believe by faith. Look at John 6:29, as it states, "Jesus answered and said unto them. This is the work of God, that ye believe on him whom He hath sent." By faith, we are able to prevail against all evil and demonic forces that will try to come against us.

We are to make preparations to be ready to defend ourselves against Satan's schemes and evil thoughts that he throws at us, making our minds his battlefield, but we must bring every thought under captivity by the word of God.

> ***Prayer:*** *Thank You, Father, for revelation of the enemy that tries to attack our minds. By faith, we will hold fast to Your word in power. Amen.*

The Second Phase Of God's Revealing Knowledge

God revealed the gospel to Paul by divine insight. He was not educated in a school of theology as preachers and teachers are today. Let us examine this concept of divine calling by revelation. God has made us stewards of the gospel that has not been established by the teaching of a man but the divine revelation of God's spirit. Jesus Christ operating on the inside of our hearts and minds gives us God's might – God's super on our natural. Let's read Galatians 1:12 (AMP), as it states, "For indeed I did not receive it from man, nor was I taught it, but I received it through a [direct] revelation of Jesus Christ." We can examine what Paul is saying by knowing how and who God is. He is a spirit, and He operates in the spirit. God works through us, in us, and with us. He does not keep us in the dark on anything. He speaks to those who are obedient to His word. The more we learn of Him and His character, the more we develop those characteristics by practice. Now we are able to hear Him clearly from within our own spirits where He abides by His saving grace because we have accepted Him as Lord and Savior of our lives.

In Galatians 1:16, Paul reveals to us that God by grace revealed "His son in [Paul] so that [Paul] might preach Him among the heathen; immediately [Paul] conferred not with flesh and blood…"

Paul is telling us that God spoke the revelation of preaching His gospel to the heathens. He did not go to the priest or any denomination. God's revealing word of His power was poured into him by divine result of God's enabling might to do what he thought was impossible.

After three years, Paul went to the other chosen disciples, mainly Peter, and stayed with them for fifteen days. I believe that during that time of fellowship, the Holy Ghost, working through Peter, encouraged and strengthened Paul by that fellowship and meditation on the word and prepared Paul's mind and spirit to be able to with withstand the darts of Satan's attacks and come out victorious as he ministered to the heathens. Paul had an assurance and witness to that supernatural ability through Jesus Christ. He lived and experienced that faith more so than any other disciple. Peter also was the one who had the faith to walk on water, and he knew firsthand about doubt and unbelief because he had to take on the nature of Christ. He had to take off the old nature and put on the new nature of Christ Jesus. Let us do the same and put on Christ Jesus as a new garment and fight the good fight of faith.

Prayer: Father, I thank You for the grace and understanding of Your wisdom by revelation knowledge through Christ Jesus. Amen.

The Third Phase Of God's Revealing Knowledge

We know that God wants us to receive the spirit of wisdom. Wisdom comes only from God. As a believer, you must pray that God gives you the wisdom you need to carry out His assignments for your life. We need a deeper understanding of God's covenant, laws, and character in order to know the will of God as it relates to our spiritual growth. God has an excellent spirit because He has a destiny plan of hope for all who love and trust Him. This relationship manifests in our prayer life and our worship. There is a difference between the two, and I will discuss this concept later on. Look at Ephesians 1:17 (AMP), as it states, "[I always pray] that the God of our Lord Jesus Christ, the Father of glory, may grant you a spirit of wisdom and of revelation [that gives you a deep and personal and intimate insight] into the true knowledge of Him [for we know the Father through the Son]." Paul reveals to us a solemn determination and desire that we should be in a close relationship with our Heavenly Father that is so spiritual and beyond the normalcy of closeness than we can ever imagine, to know God as our Father. We are to saturate our heartfelt intimacy, absorbing the precious love of God, who is in us and with us by all infallible proofs.

Love, the master portion of this spiritual connection, can only be touched through our enlightenment in worship and God's blessings through the covenant inheritance that He willingly gave us by the greatness of His mighty power. Paul manifested that trust and worship when he prayed for his brothers and sisters in Christ. Paul's unselfish prayer that denotes concern for his sisters and brothers in Christ must be our cry of perfected love that God is waiting to manifest through us so that we may inherit by grace. God revealed that precious secret to Paul, and now it is revealed to His precious children and the church. Let's clarify this confession by reading Ephesians 3:3 (AMP), as Paul states, "And that by [divine] revelation the mystery was made known to me, as I have already written in brief." Paul was chosen to be the steward of God's grace, to preach it to all men and the church for our benefits.

***Prayer:** Thank You, Father, for revealing Your grace to us so that we are fellow heirs and partakers of the blessings and promises of God through Christ Jesus. Amen.*

Our Earnest Expectations

Our total expectancy should be on God's grace and mercy. Where would we be without the gospel of Jesus Christ? Even Paul could not do such a work without the Holy Spirit inspiring, leading, and guiding him by revelation. Such are we today. We cannot walk the walk and talk the talk of living within the spirit without the assistance of the Holy Ghost. We must be sober-minded and realize that we can't live this life any way we want to without God's divine assistance. We must have the mind of Christ, given by God's grace, or we will be most miserable. This is how we get hope; we cannot determine our own paths and not expect that some divine order might have another course of destiny for us. It happens all the time. How many testimonies have you heard to the effect that someone had some fantastic plans for his or her life and something unexpectedly happened to change those plans? It's just the way life happens. Yet we know that we have hope – spiritual hope that is ever present when we have Christ in our lives. Here is a demonstration of such hope when our minds line up with God's way. Look at 1 Peter 1:13, as it states, "Wherefore gird up the loins of your mind, be sober, and hope to the end for the grace that is to be brought unto you at the revelation of Jesus Christ…"

The revelation of Jesus Christ and his love for you will put you in a mindset that will take you as far as you want to go to succeed by grace.

Your behavior will change, and your conservation will be different; you will have a desire to live like God, who wants you to live as kings and priests in the Lord.

God reveals to His children those precious promises that He gave to His son for we are His sons by inheritance. He has given us many gifts and ministries that operate by the knowledge of God and the spirit of God dwelling on the inside of us. Knowing this, we have the spiritual insight to heal, teach, preach, and even perform miracles by the power of the Holy Ghost.

Prayer: Thank You, Father, for Your grace, Your gifts, and Your love by Christ Jesus. Amen.

Grace Abides In Weakness

Grace is defined in the Hebrew as chen, which means "precious", "kindness", "pleasure", or "favor". We know that

God loves us because He has granted us favor and kindness in every area of our lives. The prophets of old knew about God's grace. Paul prayed, and God heard him and answered him. 2 Corinthians 12:9 states, "And he said my grace is sufficient for thee: for my strength is made perfect in weakness." We of ourselves can do nothing, yet God can apply His grace to our situation and bring about vengeance and divine deliverance. We must glory in our weaknesses as Paul did in order for God's supernatural power to operate in us and through us by Christ Jesus.

If you are walking upright and prayerfully with God, He will take care of you and anything that may try to come against you. As long as the spirit of God dwells on the inside of you, you are more than a conquerer. You as a conquerer win every time, not just some of the time. You win against sickness, you win against "not enough", you win against anything coming against you and your household by the power of His might. What do you need grace for? We know that grace is a gift from God because it is God's unmerited favor. So, what I can determine is that grace and favor are the same. Yet there is a measure of grace that God gives because there are different assignments that each individual has to carry out. I believe that our attitude and gratitude concerning God's gifts is based on how we receive God's divine influence in our hearts.

Remember God deals with the heart 'for out of the heart flow the issues of life.'

Let's read (Eph 4:7) "But unto every one of us is given grace according to the measure of the gift of Christ." God has given us many gifts, but many have not taken them with a spirit of gratitude or graciousness in order to receive the gifts and the manifestation of that enabling ability. God has given us everything we need to handle any situation or problem that comes up in our lives. All we have to do is measure out the gift to handle it by faith.

Prayer: Father, I thank You for the grace and the gifts You have given me. I receive them in gratitude knowing that Your grace is sufficient in weakness. Amen.

Grace That Empowers Us

We are God's helpers and laborers by grace. He has enabled us to develop and grow spiritually so that we may be equipped for service as good soldiers. Let's look at how Paul talks about what God has invested into us to create the masterpiece of His foundation by the spiritual indwelling of His divine grace formed for His people. It's depicted in 1 Corinthians 3:10, as it states, "According to the grace of God which is given unto me, as a wise masterbuilder, I have laid the foundation, and another buildeth thereon, But let every man take heed how he buildeth thereupon." The same word that God gives to one man must have the same power for another man so that the man God is building is made firm and steady. The word states that we all are fellow citizens who are of the household of God. Ephesians 2:20-21 states, "And are built upon the foundation of the apostles and prophets, Jesus Christ himself being the chief corner stone; In whom all the building fitly framed together groweth unto an holy temple in the Lord…"

We are all connected, being many yet everyone connected to one another. We are to come together and take of Christ Jesus that bread of life that makes us all partakers of eternal life, which fitly joins us together.

Paul says in Galatians 3:28, "There is neither Jew nor Greek, there is neither bond nor free, there is neither male nor female: for ye are all one in Christ Jesus." We are expected to keep the unity of peace by God's eternal spirit forever.

What we must do is ask God to give us the grace to be obedient to His word and be doers and not hearers only.

How can we escape the wrath of God if we neglect such a precious, powerful commandment of peace? Don't be deceived by the evil one into thinking that God will not defend His word. God watches over His word. He does not break His promises lest He become a liar. God is not a man that He should lie. God's divine plan of unity is for all mankind.

Prayer: Father, help us to accept Your plan of grace and to live according to Your word so that we may be empowered to experience Your grace in all that we receive and do by the power of Your might through Christ Jesus. Amen.

A Renewed Mind Trains The Tongue

The Bible teaches us that we should not be quick to correct or reprove others, knowing that we ourselves will be criticized and judged by others as well. Prepare yourself and be ready to stand by God's righteousness and not your own, deceiving yourself. Allow the teaching of the Holy Ghost to guide your thoughts so that you will speak from a place of sound and wise counsel. Let us analyze this word as it defines our topic. Look at James 3:1-2, as it states, "My brethren, be not many masters, knowing that we shall receive the greater condemnation. For in many things we offend all. If any man offends not in word, the same is a perfect man, and able also to bridle the whole body." The Lord wants us to show restraint in our speaking so that we will be able to control our entire body, our emotions, our actions and our feelings toward others. We are to control our entire life by what we speak for what we speak by faith will surely manifest in God's time. That's why we as believers should always speak the best over others and victory on our own lives lest we bring delays to God's destiny plan for our lives.

Faith here is the guiding factor that one is to incorporate in doing all things, speaking all things by faith instead of by blind judgments or confusion. God is not the Author of confusion.

We are reminded that the large ship is turned by a small helm, the horse is guided by bits in its mouth, and the tongue is a little member and boasts great things. Behold how great a matter a little fire kindles (James 3:5). Let us train our precious member that is created to be a beacon of goodness, blessing, and encouragement.

Let us tame and train this precious vessel of inspiration that can operate in the fullness of faith. Such a vessel that is able to speak life into dead things, forgiveness to the guilty, and power to the weak, for we are truly speaking spirits called and blessed by our Lord and Savior Jesus Christ by the grace of God now and forever.

Prayer: Father, thank You for the enabling power to speak, confer, and confirm Your blessings on others, giving sound understanding to Your words of life by faith through grace. Amen.

The Spiritual Mind (Prayer 1)

The man who is not born of the spirit is a natural man. Therefore, he cannot discern or understand the spiritual things nor obtain the mind of Christ. The things of God are foolishness to Him. The world's system does not operate on the same principles as God's system. The things of God are foolish to the world system and those who are not spiritual minded. They call us misfits and fools because we talk about the unseen and faith by believing and speaking those things that may seem impossible to the natural understanding to the regular mind. Yet, scriptures reveal to us that the spiritually minded man judges all things yet himself is judged of no man (1 Corinthians 1:15). We have the authority as believers to judge a matter and not feel that we have done wrong or stepped over our boundaries. We can judge a spiritual matter if we are born of Christ and have been renewed in body and spirit to the things of the Spirit by Christ Jesus. Christ came to make us leaders and ambassadors of the spiritual things on Earth. We as baptized believers should know how God works and how He deals with evil, spiritual matters.

God teaches us by example in His word. He taught His disciples to know who they were. He revealed to Paul how to discern good from evil. God proclaims in His word how the anointing operates by faith and tells us that prayer saves the sick and our faith operates by love.

The word is the key to knowing the strength of God's power by His Holy Spirit guiding our inner spirits. Our minds are connected to God's mind, not for us to teach Him, but for us to be taught by Him. The spiritually minded man's thoughts are connected enough to tap into God's unlimited supply of knowledge about God, His character, God's way of doing things, His abilities, His wisdom, and the true understanding of God's word. He works through us, with us, and in us to bring about His plans and will for His people and the church.

Prayer: Father, I thank You for the mind of Christ, that spiritual knowledge that teaches and guides me unto the power of Your resources through Your son Jesus Christ and Your words of wisdom. Amen.

The Spiritual Mind (Prayer 2)

The word tells us that we must have the mind of Christ. We are his masterpiece shaped in the character and the image of God yet, without the wisdom and knowledge of God, we are far from claiming our inheritance by faith. Let's look at one of the scriptures that shows us why we can lose out on God's promises by our own thinking. Romans 8:6 (AMP) states, "Now the mind of the flesh is death [both now and forever—because it pursues sin]; but the mind of the spirit is life and peace [the spiritual well-being that comes from walking with God—both now and forever]…"

I don't want to decide anything without the Holy Spirit leading me to such a conclusion. He is the guide, and He lets us know the wisdom of a thing before it even occurs. Listening to Him brings life and peace, and no sorrow is ever present. Let your thoughts and reasoning be submitted to God's laws and precepts, and you will never fail.

We must purpose our minds to carry out God's plans for our lives. We must not be selfish. God wants us to live lives of humbleness with a willingness to give and have minds of reciprocity. Reciprocity means to give to others as God would return mercy to you. It may not come back the same way it was given, but the end result is the same. God wants us to put on His character of eagerness to please Him.

Our lives must be an example of Jesus' life and his attitude about obeying the will of the Father. Jesus obeyed unto death, not desiring his will, but the will of the Father unto the cross. Let us look at Philippians 2:5-6 (AMP), as it states, "Have this same attitude in yourselves which was in Christ Jesus [look to him as your example in selfless humility], who, although he existed in the form and unchanging essence of God [as one with Him, possessing the fullness of all the divine attributes—the entire nature of deity], did not regard equality with God a thing to be grasped or asserted [as if he did not already possess it, or was afraid of losing it]…"

Jesus only wanted to please the Father so that God's promises would prove to be the total fullness of God's love through His son's life that he gave on the cross for all mankind.

> **Prayer:** *Thank You, Lord, for a spiritual mind so that I may be able to humble myself to Your will for my life. Amen.*

The Spiritual Mind (Prayer 3)

To have the mind of Christ brings joy and gladness. It is a delight to think about the goodness of God and all the provisions, blessings, and great gifts that He has bestowed upon His children. Psalm 104:34 says, "My meditations of Him shall be sweet: I will be glad in the Lord."

What else is there to be glad in? Surely this world cannot offer us the peace, security, hope, and love as our Heavenly Father can. Many have been deceived by the world and all imitations of life, but I am following after the purpose God has put on the inside of me. Consider all the good things God has done for you. The carnal man looks to his own devices and instruments of provision, but the spiritual man knows that God is love and provides all we need and desire. Who can give life or build a life? Only God can build us and put us back together again because He made us from the inside out. Without Him, we can do nothing. The word reveals to us in 1 Peter 4:1 (AMP), "Therefore, since Christ suffered in the flesh [and died for us], arm yourselves [like warriors] with the same purpose [being willing to suffer for doing what is right and pleasing God], because whoever has suffered in the flesh [being like-minded with Christ] is done with [intentional] sin [having stopped pleasing the world]…"

We are not guided by our selfish desires, but we have found purpose in our living for God. By His divine Holy Spirit, He has come into our hearts and minds to wash us with the word. No longer are we vessels of disgrace, but we are vessels ready for the Master's use. Now we can honestly say, as David said, "What is man, that Thou art mindful of him? And the son of man, that Thou visiteth him?" (Psalm 8:4). God's grace endures forever.

Prayer: *Thank You, Father, for teaching me to delight in Your gladness so that I may find pleasure in being obedient to Your word and pleasing You instead of pleasing the world. Amen.*

About The Author

Dr. Dorothy Sharpe: I am thrilled to say that I am a child of the King. I received Christ at the age of twelve in a Baptist Church in Greensboro, Alabama. I had come to Alabama after my mother passed in Newark, New Jersey. I was a young child and I knew that God loved me because I had heard my Grandmother say it all my life. I was living with her and she would always encourage me. As I got older, I was extremely active in the church and became a Sunday School teacher and later I became the Superintendent of Sunday School.

I became a prayer as well. God was opening up doors to me early in my life. I entered Stillman college, a private college in Tuscaloosa Alabama after

I graduated from high school. I attended Stillman from 1991-1994. I earned my English degree. I taught school for about two years and later I decided to go for my master's degree in education and school counseling at the University of West Alabama in Livingston, Alabama. I attended this school and received my Master's degree in Education and Counseling in 2000.

My first husband passed after twenty-two years, and I later married my second husband. I was doing my calling in the later years of my life as the Holy Spirit led me. At this time, I was living by faith and hope because I was depending on grants and loans to pay for my education. My husband found a job online that would take us to Florida. I was not working as a teacher then, and I decided to go with him. We stayed there for a year and he was able to get another job in San Diego, California; this was 2003. We stayed there for three years and he decided to move because of the expensiveness of the area. He took a job transfer to Chicago for a year. While in Chicago we met an incredibly famous minister at the Living Word Center. The congregation was very friendly and hospitable to us. We took ministering classes with them and joined their congregation every Sunday for worship. We decided to go to Arkansas after he wanted to purchase a home, and that is how we got to Arkansas. He worked for the government and I worked for the Pulaski County School District up until this year of 2020.

I have met so many teachers and administrators at different schools and some have even retired. I had started writing my book because I was meditating all the time on the decisions we were making about life and our livelihood. As I was working as a teacher and as a counselor, I was passionate about my work. I started writing my book in 2018, and I was terribly busy at that time in education. I took classes and got my Doctorate in Divinity because I was already ordained as my husband was a Bishop and he was working. I believe he had listened to God for his assignments, and that is how I decided to write the book. We later divorced, and I regret that. He was still searching for another high paying position, and I believe God wanted him to do the work of ministry as he was called. That is my story, and I am still going to do the work of God's guidance until he calls me home.

Our Motto
"Transforming Life Stories"

Publish Your Book With Us

Our All-Inclusive Self-Publishing Packages

100% Royalties
Professional Proofreading & Editing
Interior Design & Cover Design
Self-Publishing Tutorial & More

For Manuscript Submission or other inquiries:
www.jkenkadepublishing.com
(501) 482-JKEN

Also Available from J. Kenkade Publishing

ISBN: 978-1-944486-51-8
Visit www.amazon.com
Author: Jerry Walker

Do you find yourself asking the question, "Is there more to life than the seemingly never-ending struggle of survival?" This book answers that question with a resounding, "YES!" Jesus died to give us MORE. Jerry Walker has written this manual for Christian living that gives in-depth teaching on scripture and how to apply it to your life. Full of tools for living a life of freedom in Christ, this book will be a blessing to all who read it. Your time is now, it truly is your season!

Also Available from J. Kenkade Publishing

ISBN: 978-1-944486-73-0
Visit www.amazon.com
Author: Jerry Walker

Life shouldn't be happening to us; we should be happening to life. This is what living in excellence is all about: Using every talent, gift, capacity and revelation that God has equipped us with and reaching our fullest potential. In this 31-Day guide, you will discover how meditating and reflecting on the word of God can pull you into His divine plan for your life. Prepare to expand past mediocrity and live a life of excellence!

Also Available from J. Kenkade Publishing

ISBN: 978-1-944486-83-9
Visit www.amazon.com
Author: Apostle C.A. Turner

There's such a hunger for the things of the spirit and the supernatural. Many have decided to tap into the dark side in order to understand more about the Supernatural and the things of the spirit. One of the reasons for this I believe, is because the church as a whole has lost the desire to see a move of God validated by his power with miracles, signs, and wonders. It's my desire and prayer that this information will activate you in ways you never dreamed as you apply it to your spiritual life.

Also Available from J. Kenkade Publishing

ISBN: 978-1-944486-65-5
Visit www.amazon.com
Author: Ramona Freeman

"Prayer: My Incense to God" is a composition of prayers created by the author over the years for various topics. The purpose of this prayer manual is to set a foundation of prayer and intercession according to the Word of God, to establish prayer in every home, city, state, and nation, and to pray the will of God in order to see His kingdom come on Earth as it is in Heaven (Matthew 6:10).

www.ingramcontent.com/pod-product-compliance
Lightning Source LLC
Chambersburg PA
CBHW061449300426
44114CB00014B/1904